THE WORKS OF SIR JOHN CLANVOWE

THE WORKS OF SIR JOHN CLANVOWE

Edited by V.J.Scattergood

Published by D.S.Brewer Ltd
and Rowman and Littlefield

Published by D.S.Brewer Ltd
240 Hills Road Cambridge
and P.O.Box 24 Ipswich IP1 1JJ

ISBN 0 85991 010 5

First published in the U.S.A. 1975 by
Rowman and Littlefield Totowa N.J. 07512

Library of Congress Cataloging in Publication Data

Scattergood, V.J. comp.
  The works of Sir John Clanvowe

  Contains 2 Middle English works, The boke of Cupide
and The two ways; the 1st work, of uncertain authorship,
has been traditionally included in the Chaucer canon,
but in recent scholarship has been attributed to J.Clan-
vowe, T.Clanvowe, or R.Roos. Cf.V.J.Scattergood, Authorship of The boke of Cupide, in Anglia, v.82.
  Bibliography: p.
  1. English poetry— Middle English, 1100-1500.
I. Chaucer, Geoffrey, d.1400. Spurious and doubtful
works. Boke of Cupide. II. Clanvowe, Sir John, 1341?-
1391. Boke of Cupide. III. Clanvowe, Sir Thomas, fl.1400.
Boke of Cupide. IV. Roos, Sir Richard, 1410 (ca.)-1482.
Boke of Cupide. V. Clanvowe, Sir John, 1341?-1391. The
two ways. 1975. VI. Boke of Cupide. 1975.

PR1203.S3   821'.1'08   75-2355
ISBN 0-87471-688-8

Printed in Great Britain by
Redwood Burn Limited
Trowbridge & Esher

CONTENTS

Preface   7
Abbreviations   8

INTRODUCTION   9

I THE BOKE OF CUPIDE

i   Literary Background and Date   9
ii   Manuscripts and Texts   14
iii Language, Dialect and Versification   16

II THE TWO WAYS

i   Religious Context   18
ii   Manuscripts   21

III SIR JOHN CLANVOWE

i   Writings   22
ii   Life   25

Notes to the Introduction   28
A Note on the Texts   32

THE BOKE OF CUPIDE   33

THE TWO WAYS   57

COMMENTARY

I THE BOKE OF CUPIDE   81
II THE TWO WAYS   86

SELECT BIBLIOGRAPHY   90

GLOSSARY   92

PREFACE

I FIRST BECAME interested in the texts here edited over ten years ago, and some of my findings have been publish-ed elsewhere (see bibliography). For this book, however, the material and the conclusions have been looked at again in the light of recent research, and augmented and modified where necessary.

I should like to express my gratitude to the librari-ans and staff of the University Libraries of Birmingham and Bristol, who have supplied me with books over several years; and to the British Museum, the University Library Cambridge and the Bodleian Library Oxford for allowing me to consult manuscripts in their possession.

In particular, I should like to thank Derek Brewer, who, as teacher, graduate supervisor and now publisher, has given me unfailing encouragement and constructive advice.

ABBREVIATIONS

Cal. Close Rolls	*Calendar of Close Rolls*
Cal. Pat. Rolls	*Calendar of Patent Rolls*
EETS OS / ES	Early English Text Society Original Series / Extra Series
MED	*The Middle English Dictionary* ed. H. Kurath, S.M.Kuhn, J.Reidy, Michigan 1954 (in progress)
MLN	*Modern Language Notes*
OED	*The Oxford English Dictionary* ed. J.A.H.Murray, H.Bradley, W.A.Craigie, C.T.Onions, Oxford 1933
PMLA	*Publications of the Modern Language Association of America*
RS	Rolls Series
SATF	Société des Anciens Textes Français

INTRODUCTION

SIR JOHN CLANVOWE claims the attention of literary
critics and scholars, and of historians, alike. By turns
soldier, administrator, diplomat and chamber knight at
the courts of Edward III and Richard II, Clanvowe is
constantly associated in the records with men who appear
to have formed a prominent group of earnest, secular
intellectual knights who were interested in literature
and religion— Lewis Clifford, Richard Sturry, Thomas
Latimer, William Nevill, John Montague and John Cheyne,
a group with which Chaucer himself appears to have had
close relationships. What distinguishes Clanvowe from
the others is that he was a writer of some ability; two
of his works have survived: *The Boke of Cupide* (if the
hypothesis formulated below is accepted), perhaps the
earliest and one of the best poems to show the influence
of Chaucer; and *The Two Ways*, a religious treatise which
provides evidence for the degree and nature of Clanvowe's interest in Lollardy.

I THE BOKE OF CUPIDE

i *Literary Background and Date*

The Boke of Cupide is a poem in the tradition made
familiar by Chaucer's *Parliament of Fowls*, with which it
shows close and deep familiarity. It is a dream-vision
incorporating a debate between the Nightingale and the
Cuckoo about the nature of love. The occasion of the
poem's composition is difficult to determine and there
have been different theories about this. But in genre
and subject matter, such is the poem's aptness for a
courtly audience, and such its connections with St.
Valentine's Day (78-80, 281-282), that it is reasonable
to suppose that, like the *Parliament of Fowls*, it was
intended as a literary celebration of this festival. The
ornate compliment to "the Quene / At Wodestok" (284-285)

9

makes it almost certain that it was intended for the royal court.

D.E.Lampe[1] has recently argued, on the basis of the traditional associations of the two birds involved, that the poem is much more than a *divertimento*. The cuckoo is "the betrayed husband, the cuckold...and the love that he is attacking is adulterous love". The nightingale, Lampe argues, is more complex: one tradition associates the bird with profane, adulterous love (which is how the cuckoo describes her), another makes her the representative of divine love or loyal married love. The narrator, who is "olde and vnlusty" (37), he takes to be "a comic old buffoon lover" and as a remedy for his lovesickness the nightingale recommends marriage, represented by another symbol of constancy, the "fresshe flour daysye" (243). To me, however, the poem does not seem to say this, and a more precise indication of the author's intention may be suggested by a consideration of some of the sources of his inspiration.

It is unlikely that *The Boke of Cupide* is derived from any single source. No debate in which the main opponents are a cuckoo and a nightingale exists. The central motif, the belief among lovers

"That hit wer good to her the nyghtyngale
  Rather then the leude cukkow syng" (49-50),

appears, from the words "tokenyng" and "comvne tale" (47-48), to be based on a proverb[2]. Two proverbs such as may be alluded to here have been recorded, though neither can be traced back to the fourteenth century[3].

But the poem demonstrably owes much to literary sources. The association of the nightingale with love and the opposition of the cuckoo to love appear together in two French poems. In lines 1-416 of the early fourteenth-century "love-vision", *La Messe des Oiseaus et li Plais des Chanonesses et des Grises Nonains*[4], the poet Jean de Condé dreams that one day in a forest he sees Venus enthroned receiving the adoration of the gathered

10

birds. It is a familiar parody following the offices of the Mass but celebrating erotic love. As the nightingale sings the Gloria the cuckoo, his enemy, interrupts and bids him be silent. This annoys the devotees of love and the cuckoo is chased off:

"...*li autre oisiel l'encachierent*
Et durement le manechierent
Si s'en fui tous estourdis..." (146-148)

[...the other birds drove him away and harshly
threatened him so that, defeated, he took flight...]

much as the cuckoo is driven away by the narrator of *The Boke of Cupide* (216-220). But thinking to be revenged he flies back over the worshippers crying "*Tout cuku*" (310) with the predictable result:

"*Il en fait maint cuer irascu*
De ce k'il lor dist tel laidure" (311-312)

[He makes many a heart angry with the ugly
things he says to them]

and the hawk drives him off once more until he takes refuge in a hollow tree. Venus then explains the cuckoo's evil nature.

In Eustache Deschamps' ballade "*En ce douls temps...*"[5] the poet walks out one May morning "*Car a Amours vouls rendre mon salu*" [Since I wish to give my greeting to Love] but he hears no pleasant birdsong "*...seulement le chant du cucu*" [only the song of the cuckoo]. The poet's reaction to this indicates that the cuckoo's song was regarded as inauspicious for lovers:

"*Adonc me pris forment a esbahir*
Et de son chant durement me courcay
Qu'en lieu d'amer me rouvoit a hair." (9-11)

[Then I began to be greatly troubled and ran quickly
from his song for instead of loving I was provoked
to hate.]

11

The spring landscape no longer seems beautiful to the poet and he falls into despair, but Pity encourages him not to be too disheartened, because the future may often bring a change of fortune. However, the ballade ends on a sad note:

> *"Car l'en oit poy rossignol, papegay,*
> *Fors seulement que le chant du cucu."* (23-24)

> [For one hears little of the nightingale or the parrot, only the song of the cuckoo.]

The main literary inspiration of *The Boke of Cupide*, however, is Chaucer[6]. Whether or not this author used the *F Prologue to the Legend of Good Women* is a matter of dispute[7], but it is fairly clear that he used *The Parliament of Fowls*. In terms of genre they have much in common: each is a "love-vision" drawing on St Valentine's Day beliefs and each concerns a debate between birds about love. A faintly comic first person narrator involves himself in the action of each poem. Verbal parallels are harder to establish, but both poems end in the same way with joyous birdsong which awakes the narrator. Lines 693-695 of *The Parliament of Fowls*

> "And with the shoutyng, when the song was do
> That foules maken at here flyght away
> I wok"

may have provided the suggestion for *The Boke of Cupide*, 288-290. The antithetical nature of love,

> "That bringes in to hertis remembraunce
> A maner ease, medled with grevaunce
> And lusty thoghtes ful of grete longynge", (28-30)

central to *The Boke of Cupide*, is also one of Chaucer's concerns (see lines 127-140), though his debate is more complex and philosophical.

The one passage in *The Knight's Tale* which caught Clanvowe's attention deals with a remarkably similar topic. For his opening couplet he quotes Theseus on the power of love, almost as if it were a *sententia*:

"The god of love, a, benedicite!
  How myghty and how greet a lord is he!" (1785-1786)

Then he expands Chaucer's couplet

"For he kan maken, at his owene gyse,
  Of everich herte as that hym list divyse" (1789-1790)

into a series of antithetical statements about the power
of love to alter human fortunes and cause happiness and
sadness indiscriminately (3-20). This is a common enough
topic certainly, but there is more than a hint of it in
the relevant passage from *The Knight's Tale*. The ex-
perienced Theseus muses on the power of love which had
led the young knights Palamon and Arcite, who "myghte
han lyved in Thebes roially" (1793), to a wood near
Athens "hyder bothe for to dye" (1797); he wonders at
the paradoxical nature of love which has repaid their
service by making them "blede" and by betraying them
into the hands of "hir mortal enemy"; yet he recognises
also that love gives them hopes of some satisfaction:

"And yet they wenen for to been ful wyse
  That serven love, for aught that may bifalle."
                                              (1804-1805)

   Like the two knights, the narrator of *The Boke of
Cupide* persists in hoping, against all reason, for
success in love: he is "olde and vnlusty" (37), he walks
out at an unlucky time (55 and note), he hears the inauspicious cuckoo sing first (90) and, if either bird
can be said to win the argument, it is the cuckoo (209
and note). The narrator is rewarded for his devotion
with kind words, an injunction to constancy (241-246)
and promises (234-235). He is himself the slightly
ridiculous, suffering but ever hopeful subject of his
own poem, the perfect example (36-40) of a man caught by
the irresistible but ambivalent power of love. *The Boke
of Cupide* is a wryly self-mocking treatment of the

13

touching irrational folly that love is capable of producing in those old enough and wise enough to know better.

On the basis of its borrowings from Chaucer a tentative date may be assigned to *The Boke of Cupide*. *The Parliament of Fowls* is usually dated 1382-1383, and *The Knight's Tale* within the period 1382-1386. If there are also borrowings from the *F Prologue to the Legend of Good Women* its earliest date would be after 1386; and, if Sir John Clanvowe were the author of the poem, it must have been written before 1391, when he died. This would fit well enough with the evidence of the language, making *The Boke of Cupide* not only one of the earliest Chaucerian pieces but also somewhat earlier than has hitherto been thought[8].

ii Manuscripts and Texts

The Boke of Cupide survives in five manuscript copies: Fairfax 16, Bodley 638, Arch. Selden B 24 and Tanner 346 in the Bodleian Library, Oxford[9]; and in Cambridge University Library Ff. 1.6[10]. These are all well-known Chaucer manuscripts and it is not surprising that *The Boke of Cupide* also appeared in the 1532 edition of Chaucer by Thynne and in subsequent editions. Largely as a result of this, the poem was, until the late nineteenth century, attributed to Chaucer.

Fairfax 16 (F) is written in a neat professional hand of the mid-fifteenth century. Amongst other things it contains poems by Chaucer, Gower, Hoccleve and Lydgate and the lyrics attributed to William de la Pole, Duke of Suffolk. *The Boke of Cupide* appears on ff.35v-39v. The flyleaf bears the date 1450 and the arms of the Stanley family appear on f.14v, so the manuscript may perhaps have been commissioned by Thomas, first Lord Stanley (1406-1459). In the early seventeenth century it perhaps belonged to the Wingfield family of Northampton and perhaps also to John Stow, before it was bought by Charles Fairfax in 1650. The text of *The Boke of Cupide* is neatly and carefully written, but there are a few errors (see variants to lines 140, 141, 142, 153, 286, 287) of the type which could easily have been corrected by a scribe in the habit of checking his work.

Bodley 638 (B) is defective at beginning and end and is otherwise somewhat damaged. Nothing is known for sure of its owners[11]. It contains several of Chaucer's shorter poems and others by Hoccleve. *The Boke of Cupide* appears on ff.11v-16r. The manuscript was written in a coarse and untidy way by one man, and rubricated by someone who has worked his name— 'Lity' or 'Lyty'— into the colophons on ff.4v, 7r, 38r, 45v, 141r, 209v. The text was checked and corrected by both scribe and rubricator and only two minor slips have escaped notice (see variants to lines 26, 184).

Arch. Selden B 24 (S) contains poems by Chaucer, Hoccleve and Lydgate, and the text of *The Boke of Cupide*, which is incomplete, appears on ff.138v-141v. A note on f.120r refers to James IV, who came to the Scottish throne in 1488, and another on f.230v indicates the book was owned by Henry Lord Sinclair[12], who died at Flodden in 1513, so the manuscript was apparently composed between these dates. The spelling is Scottish and the texts are sophisticated, but the manuscript is carefully written with no obvious mechanical errors.

Tanner 346 (T), written in several fifteenth-century hands, contains poems by Chaucer, Hoccleve and Lydgate. *The Boke of Cupide* appears on ff.97r-101r and *The Envoy to Alison* is appended to it. The manuscript perhaps belonged to John Greystoke (died 1500-1501), sixth lord of the Yorkshire baronial family. The text has many errors: lines 201-205, 217-219, 224-225 are omitted; the second halves of lines 156 and 157 are transposed; and there are several other errors (see variants to lines 89, 147, 149, 185, 281).

Ff.1.6 (Ff) includes many short anonymous pieces as well as poems by Chaucer, Gower, Hoccleve and Lydgate. Some twenty-four different hands are responsible for writing the items. Originally the manuscript belonged to the Findern family of south Derbyshire. *The Boke of Cupide*, which appears on ff.22r-28r, is written in a neat, firm mid-fifteenth-century hand. The scribe made running corrections, but several errors have escaped notice (see variants to lines 21, 58, 79, 127, 158, 160, 257).

Thynne's 1532 Edition of Chaucer (Th) contains a text of *The Boke of Cupide* which is based on a text very similar to that in Tanner 346. It shares the omissions and transpositions of lines in that text and it also appends *The Envoy to Alison*.

The six texts of *The Boke of Cupide* may be classified as two groups: F.B. and Ff.S.T.Th.[13] The relationship between F and B is clear: they share more than 30 common errors. It may be that they derive from a common exemplar; but neither can have been copied from the other, for F has 17 unique errors and B has six. There is no such close correspondence between Ff.S.T.Th, but they have in common 17 errors. Within this group of four, Ff.T.Th. have more than 60 instances of common error, though some of these occur after S. breaks off. S.T.Th. have 6 instances of common error. The correspondence between the Ff. and S. texts and the other texts of this group is not great, for Ff. has more than 50 unique errors and S. more than 130; in the case of S. the scribe seems deliberately to have re-written copy which must have seemed to him defective metrically, because he did not count grammatical final -*e* as a syllable. The T.Th. texts, are however, closely related and have more than 50 common errors. Neither is copied from the other since each has about a dozen unique errors, but they could derive from a common exemplar.

iii Language, Dialect and Versification

The linguistic features of *The Boke of Cupide* have previously been examined and only a few points are worthy of note. Perhaps most interesting is the extent of the preservation of grammatical final -*e*. There are more than 120 occurrences (not counting those at the ends of lines) but conclusions based on this may be drawn only tentatively. The use of final -*e* in the poetry of Chaucer and his followers is not consistent and it may to some extent have been used as a metrical device. Most scholars, however, consider this author's use of final -*e* to be as conservative as Chaucer's, and it is the opinion of C.E.Ward that it is similar to Chaucer's usage within the period 1387-1391[14].

A few features do, however, serve to distinguish this author's language from that of Chaucer, though basically he writes in the same London dialect. The rhymes *vpon/ronne/mon* (81-85) show in *mon* an example of OE ă/ŏ before a nasal occurring as *o*— usually a West Midland feature, though the rhymes at 133-134 and 223-224 are non-West Midland. Some non-Chaucerian items of vocabulary appear— *grede* (135) and *lyther* (14)— but, though these do appear in West Midland authors, they can occur in other dialects as well.

The versification of *The Boke of Cupide* is of some interest, for an uncommon stanza form, a quintain of usually decasyllabic lines rhyming AABBA, here makes its first appearance in English. It has been suggested that the form was developed from the tail-rhyme stanza or from such combinations of rhyme as are found in French roundels and virelays[15]. But the stanza also existed in independent form around this time in poems by Deschamps, Froissart and Chartier, and may have been derived from there[16]. It was certainly recognised as a formal metre later by the author of the anonymous *L'Art Rhetorique pour Rimer en Plusieurs Sortes de Rimes*:

> *"Je suis de cinq piez*
> *Ainsi enlassez;*
> *Cinquain m'appell' on;*
> *En dit de chancon*
> *Suis souvent logez"*[17],

and was frequently used by Dunbar.

Any analysis of the verse of *The Boke of Cupide* is

complicated by possible textual corruption and the
problem of final -*e*, but it is safe to say that the
basic measure is the decasyllabic iambic line; e.g. 109,
188, 253. The most frequent variation on this is the
addition of an unstressed syllable at the end of the
line; e.g. 67, 74, 191, 212. Perhaps the most distinctive feature of the poem, though, is the number of 'head-
less' lines; e.g. 50: these are often encountered in
dialogue; e.g. 146. This licence is not uncommon;
Chaucer uses it, but sparingly. Inversion of the rhythm
occurs in the first foot of some lines— e.g. 24, 283—
and some lines have distinctive octosyllabic patterns—
e.g. 152, 202.

II THE TWO WAYS

i Religious Context

The Two Ways is important for the evidence it provides
about the extent and nature of support for Lollardy
among the knightly classes of the late fourteenth century. The chroniclers Knighton (under 1382) and Walsing-
ham (under 1387, 1395 and 1399)[18] mention in all ten
knights, including Sir John Clanvowe, who were Lollards
or supporters of Lollards; but their statements have
been subjected to a good deal of scholarly questioning.
In 1913 W.T.Waugh[19] brought forward evidence to deny the
heresy of all except Sir Thomas Latimer: the evidence
against the others was, he argued, too slight to be
significant and, moreover, some of the knights could be
shown to have engaged in activities such as crusading
which were condemned by Wycliffe.
    Recently, however, K.B.McFarlane[20], in an important
re-examination of the problem, reached very different
conclusions. There is no case against three of the
knights, Sir John Trussell, Sir John Peachey and Sir
Reynold Hilton— in fact, the last named probably did not
exist. But the other seven seem to have formed a loose
group. They were all attached to the court by the early

1380s and all made themselves scarce during the crisis of 1386-1388. All were quite rich and several held land and positions of influence in South Wales and the Marches; most were diplomats and men of culture; and they appear to have known each other quite well. That these knights formed an identifiable group with common interests may in part explain why the chroniclers should have thought of them together; it does not, in itself, prove that they were Lollards, though it is corroborative evidence.

The precise evidence exists elsewhere. McFarlane shows that Latimer was protecting Lollards in Northamptonshire in 1388-1389; in 1387 Sir William Nevill, Clanvowe's close friend, was, in his capacity as constable of Nottingham Castle, protecting no less a heretic than Nicholas Hereford[21]. The unusual wills of Latimer, Sir Lewis Clifford and Sir John Cheyne are further evidence: each is in English, each gives extravagant emphasis to the testator's worthlessness in ·similar verbal formulas, each is strongly contemptuous of the body and has strict injunctions against funeral pomp. Two of the executors of Clifford's will were Sir John Oldcastle, leader of the Lollard rising of 1414, and his prominent supporter, Richard Colefox.

It is known that Clanvowe was associated with Lollard sympathisers, but his treatise is the only surviving piece of writing (other than wills) known to have come from the knights. It is important in that it provides specific evidence for the religious views of one of them. *The Two Ways* is not so much a Lollard tract as a treatise which shows some sympathy with Lollard positions. It is not doctrinally polemical: it attacks neither the tenets nor the organisation of the medieval Church. It has nothing to say about papal and priestly authority, the necessity for Church endowment, the validity of confession, or the use of pilgrimages, indulgences or images. The controversial doctrine of the real presence is never mentioned. Perhaps the most significant fact about the treatise is that the Church

and its teaching are ignored. The treatise seeks simply
to show Christians how to avoid the "broode way" that
leads to hell and how to enter the "nargh way" that
leads to heaven. To attain salvation one needs to lead
a good life based on biblical teaching (95-105), and the
Bible is referred to frequently Clanvowe rejects the
values of the world: though he had been a soldier, he
condemns war and the slaughter and destruction it pro-
duces (484-488); though for long a courtier, he re-
pudiates the rich excesses of courts and their pre-
occupation with worldly attainment (489-499). All these
attitudes were broadly shared by the Lollards. At times
his language is similar to that of the Lollard wills
(360-383)[22]. Moreover, in one passage Clanvowe takes
upon himself and others like him the word *loller* (512)
meaning 'loafer' or 'idler', a term often deliberately
and scornfully misapplied to Lollards. *The Two Ways* is a
non-controversial but serious-minded and practical
secular response to the doctrines of the most controversial contemporary religious movement.

Clanvowe's biblical learning does not appear to have
been very deep or very broad. Except for two passages
(349-353; 626-642), which derive ultimately but possibly
not directly from the Old Testament and Apocrypha, he
seems to have used only Psalms, the Gospels and the
Epistles. Though on occasions he paraphrases (97-100;
742-779), his reference is usually fairly precise. He
does not appear to have used the Wycliffite Bible. At
times his phraseology is close to that of the Vulgate,
but in two places it looks as though Clanvowe's versions
are the result of misreadings of an English translation.
The rendering of I Timothy, vi, 9, "*quae mergunt homines
in interitum et perditionem*" as "þe whiche drawen men to
manslauȝtre and also bryngen men to los of body and of
soule" (467-468) suggests that Clanvowe was using an
English version which had "drownen" for *mergunt*: "drawen"
is perhaps the result of a misreading, a confusion
between *a* and *o* and a failure to notice the contraction
mark for *n*. Similarly, the rendering of I John, v, 3

20

"*Haec est enim caritas Dei, ut mandata ejus custodiamus*"
as "it is the charge of God þat we keepe hise comaundementʒ" (690-692) looks like the result of a misreading
of "charyte" (for *caritas*) as "charge". Of course, these
could be errors made by a copyist from Clanvowe's own
text; but if so they are not simple mechanical errors,
and some "editing" must have been involved.

ii Manuscripts

Two copies of *The Two Ways* are known at present: a complete text in University College Oxford MS 97 and a
fragmentary copy of lines 770-870 in British Museum
MS Additional 22283.

    University College Oxford MS 97 (U) is composite[23].
A table of contents on ff.4r-4v lists only the items
from f.85r onwards and these texts evidently once formed
an entity in their own right. Most of these items are on
devotional subjects and are written in English prose,
but the manuscript up to this point consists of items in
Latin. Sir John Clanvowe's *The Two Ways* appears on
ff.114r-123v and is written in the same clear hand as
that responsible for most of the English items. This
part of the manuscript seems to have been put together
around 1400: on ff.170r-171r appears the will of Robert
Folkingham dated 1399; on ff.176r-179v a skeleton
chronicle from the beginning of the world to 1399; on
ff.174v-175v the grant of a furred robe dated 10th
April 1400. The recipient was one W.C., whose initials
appear again in a grant on ff.171r-172r, and who is
elsewhere said to have been presented to the parish of
P. in the diocese of Worcester on 15th October 1392 by
Sir William Beauchamp, whose clerk he was. McFarlane
identifies W.C. as William Counter, rector of Pirton,
Worcestershire, whose patron was Sir William Beauchamp.
Since Beauchamp was closely connected with Clanvowe and
his friends, William Counter as his clerk "in 1392...
was in a position to have access to the original
homily"[24].

British Museum MS Additional 22283 (Simeon MS) (A) is a
large vellum folio book now of 172 leaves but originally
much bigger: 207 of its original leaves have been lost,
including those which contained the greater part of *The
Two Ways*. What remains of the treatise appears on f.116r
col.a. The manuscript contains religious pieces in verse
and prose, nearly all in English. It includes some items
also found in Bodleian MS Eng. Poet. a 1 (Vernon MS) to
which it is obviously closely related: Kari Sajavaara
suggests they were copied from the same exemplar[25]. A
note on f.38r to the effect that "John Scryvein" copied
part of it for "Thomas Heneley" also appears in Vernon
MS f.239v. Miss Hope Emily Allen has found records of a
John Scryvein of Lichfield who owned property in London
in the late fourteenth century, and a residentiary canon
of Lichfield called Thomas Hanley who was admitted to a
prebend of Gaia Major Lichfield on 27th January 1389.
Additional 22283 may therefore come from Lichfield[26]. On
palaeographic and linguistic evidence it may be dated
about 1400; since it includes Sir John Clanvowe's treatise, it must be after 1391. Five other pieces besides
The Two Ways appear in both University College Oxford
MS 97 and Additional 22283 so there may have been some
connection between the two manuscripts, though exactly
what it was is not certain.

III SIR JOHN CLANVOWE

i Writings

Sir John Clanvowe's authorship of *The Two Ways* is hardly
open to doubt: in the first line his name is clearly
given and the statement that he died abroad after cross-
ing the Mediterranean is confirmed by other evidence.
But there is no such certainty about *The Boke of Cupide*,
which has been variously attributed to Chaucer, to Sir
Thomas Clanvowe and to Sir Richard Roos as well as to
Sir John Clanvowe, who I think wrote it[27].
     The basis for this hypothesis rests on the colophon

22

reading *Explicit Clanvowe* following the Ff.1.6. copy of
the poem. W.W.Skeat[28], who first noticed this, and subsequent scholars, took it to refer to the author. In
1954, however, R.H.Robbins[29] argued that the "Clanvowe"
referred to was a copyist, like others whose names
appear in the manuscript, who had copied this particular
poem into what was originally "a blank commonplace book".
But Ff.1.6. does not have the uniformity one might ex-
pect from a commonplace book. The pages differ in size
and texture and the outer leaves of some sections are
dirty and worn as if they had once formed the covers of
separate booklets. Indeed ff.22-28, which contain *The
Boke of Cupide*, look as if they had originally an independent existence: they are written by none of the
copyists responsible for other items, but in a hand,
slightly earlier than most, which is nowhere else to be
found in the manuscript. Furthermore, the *Explicit Clanvowe* colophon does not look like a copyist's signature:
no copyist called "Clanvowe" has been found, and the tag
Salue stella maris mater firma dei vite on f.28r following the colophon, which Robbins thought was "the kind...
a scribe might add after completing his work", does not
appear to be in the hand that copied the poem.

If "Clanvowe" is indeed the name of the author, it
remains to decide between the various contemporaries who
might have written such a poem. The claims of Sir Thomas
Clanvowe, perhaps the son or, more likely, the nephew of
Sir John, have been variously set out[30], but the evidence
to support them has been shown to be not very substan-
tial[31]. Sir John Clanvowe is a much more likely candid-
ate. Since the use of final *-e* in *The Boke of Cupide*
corresponds roughly to Chaucer's for the period 1387-
1391, it is reasonable to assume that the author was
probably a contemporary, such as Sir John Clanvowe who
was born about 1341. If he were the author of the poem
he would, assuming the dates suggested above are correct,
have been between 45 and 50 when he wrote it, old enough,
that is, to have been able to refer to himself as 'olde
and vnlusty' (37). Since he was so frequently at court,

23

Sir John would have been capable of writing in the London dialect, and, since he was probably born in Herefordshire and subsequently had much to do with the West Midlands, the *mon* form at line 85 would not have been strange to him. He was also well enough known at court to have been in a position to compliment 'the Quene / At Wodestok' (284-285), a probable reference to Anne of Bohemia. As early as 1st May 1380 Sir John knew Chaucer: he was a witness along with Nevill, Beauchamp and two others to Cecily Chaumpaigne's general release of Chaucer "for all actions of rape of her or otherwise"[32]. If Sir John Clanvowe were indeed a friend of Chaucer in the 1380s, what could be more natural than that he should know and echo his famous contemporary's poems? Finally, the existence of *The Two Ways* indisputably proves Sir John a man of some literary ability; and that his interest was not confined to religious prose is indicated by an impromptu attack (493-499) on an aspect of contemporary writing which he disliked.

There is evidence too, of a corroborative sort, in that the Lollard knights and their friends were exceptionally literary. According to the chronicler Creton[33], Sir John Montague

"...*faisoit balades & chancons*
Rondeaulx & lais
Tresbien et bel,"

though these presumably French poems are now lost or unidentifiable. Sir Guichard d'Angle, in whose will Sir John Clanvowe is mentioned, numbered among his friends Oton de Graunson, Chaucer and Deschamps[34]. Sir Lewis Clifford took ballades by Deschamps to England for Chaucer[35]. Sir Philip de la Vache, who is mentioned with Clanvowe in several documents, is addressed directly in comradely terms by Chaucer in his poem *Truth*[36]. Sir Richard Sturry, who is associated with Clanvowe as early as 1378, must have known Froissart quite well[37]. There is also evidence that some of Clanvowe's group possessed books: Sturry had a *Roman de la Rose*[38], and in 1393 the

24

Duchess of York left her book of "vices and virtues" to Clifford[39]. Sir Philip de la Vache mentions no books in his will, but his widow had a commentary on St Matthew's Gospel and a "Pore Caytife" in English[40]. It is clear from this that McFarlane is right when he points out that "...not all the books were of an improving character. If these men were Lollards, they shared many of the worldly tastes for which the court at all times, and not least under Richard II, was famous"[41]. Evidently they did not find secular and religious tastes in literature incompatible, so it is perhaps not too surprising that the two pieces of writing which seem to be by Sir John Clanvowe differ to such an extent in subject matter.

ii Life

Quite a lot is known about Sir John Clanvowe. His ancestors were Welsh and owned land in Herefordshire and Radnor which Sir John inherited. He was probably the son of John Clanvowe, who was MP for Herefordshire in 1348 and esquire of the king's household in 1349. Since this man's heir was a minor in 1361 but had evidently reached his majority in 1362, when with five others he entered into recognisances towards the king for £1,000 to be levied in Herefordshire, it appears that Sir John Clanvowe was born in 1341[42].

Like most young men of comparable status and ambition, Clanvowe fought in the French campaigns. In 1364 he was on military service in Brittany[43]. He was at the skirmish at Lussac Bridge when the famous Sir John Chandos was killed and, according to Froissart, fought bravely[44]. Clanvowe and Nevill were both in the army of Sir Robert Knollys which, in 1370, invaded northern France[45]. Clanvowe, Clifford and Latimer also took part in John of Gaunt's expedition of 1373-1374[46]; and in 1378, again as a member of Gaunt's army in France, Clanvowe shared the command of 120 men with Nevill, Sturry and Philip de la Vache[47]. These campaigns were not militarily very important but for the successful participants they provided a lucrative income from booty and ransoms.

By this time, though, Clanvowe had more secure sources of wealth. In 1373 he was knight bachelor in the service of Humphrey Bohun, Earl of Hereford, from whom he received a life annuity of £40[48]. On the Earl's death on 16th January 1373 Clanvowe passed into the service of Edward III who, on 15th June 1373, granted him an additional life annuity of £50[49]. Thereafter he is found in connection with the court. He seems to have been of Gaunt's party: he received a gift from Gaunt in 1373 and was, with Nevill, among the mainpernors of William, Lord Latimer, who was impeached at the Good Parliament in 1376[50]. On Edward III's death, both Clanvowe and Nevill passed into Richard II's household and in 1381 both received 100 marks life annuity as knights of the Chamber[51].

Between 1381 and 1385 Clanvowe is mainly concerned with Wales and the Marches. He is frequently mentioned on commissions to investigate disturbances and to keep peace in these areas, and is the recipient of several grants of money and land— presumably for his services. The largest of these were the grants for life of custody of Haverford Castle, the stewardship of its lordship, and the keepership of the forests of Snowdon and Merioneth[52]. In 1385, however, he was ordered, with Nevill and others, to inspect the forts and castles of the Scottish Marches, and he seems to have been with Richard II on the inglorious Scottish expedition of this year[53].

In the winter of 1385 he left domestic affairs for European diplomacy. With Beauchamp and others he was empowered to treat for peace with the French and, on his return from France, he was among the ambassadors commissioned to settle terms between Portugal and John of Gaunt, who was organising an expedition to claim the throne of Castile[54]. It is clear from the nature of his duties and the extent of his rewards that Clanvowe was an intimate and trusted member of Richard II's "court party", so it is not surprising that when the control of the government passed to the Lords Appellant his successful career should have been interrrupted. His name is virtually absent from the records from the autumn of 1386 to the winter of 1388. He seems to have stood by Richard in the crisis[55] but he escaped the vengeance of the Merciless Parliament.

When Richard was his own master again, Clanvowe's career resumed its former course. In the summer of 1389 he was one of the ambassadors who negotiated a three years' truce with France. In the same year he was appointed, with Nevill, Clifford and others, to negotiate with the Duke of Brittany, and was granted £100 for his expenses on these various journeys[56]. In 1390 he is mentioned on a commission to the Welsh Marches to enquire into what lands reverted to the crown on the death of John, Lord Hastings[57], and later in the same year he joined Nevill and others on Louis of Bourbon's crusade against the Moors of Tunis. The expedition was a disaster, but the English knights seem to have acquitted themselves well and returned with the other survivors to Genoa[58].

In early 1391 Clanvowe is found once more in France on peace negotiations, which were successful, and Froissart says that the English ambassadors returned via Calais and Dover to London to give their report to the king[59]. After this nothing is known until the account of his and Nevill's deaths near Constantinople in October 1391. What they were doing there is uncertain: a pilgrimage would seem a more likely explanation than a crusade. The author of the continuation of Higden's *Polychronicon* throws no light on the matter, though he appears otherwise to have precise information: according to him Sir John Clanvowe died on 17th October and Sir William Nevill, who out of grief for his dead friend refused to take food, died two days later. He concludes with their eulogy: *"Erant isti milites inter Anglicos famosi viri nobiles et strenui ac etiam de genere claro producti"* [These soldiers were, among the English, famous men, noble and vigorous, and furthermore born of illustrious families][60].

NOTES

1 In *The Art and Age of Geoffrey Chaucer*, ed. J.Gardner and N.Joost, 1967, pp.49-62.

2 B.J. and H.W.Whiting, *Proverbs, Sentences and Proverbial Phrases*, 1968, N 111.

3 *The Oxford Dictionary of Proverbs*, ed. W.G.Smith and Janet E.Heseltine, 2nd rev. edition, 1948, pp.452, 651.

4 ed. A.Scheler, *Dits et Contes de Baudouain de Condé et de son fils Jean de Condé*, 1866, III 1.

5 ed. Marquis de Queux de St Hilaire and Gaston Raynaud, *Oeuvres Complètes de Eustache Deschamps*, SATF 1878-1903, III 296 (No.476).

6 Chaucer's works are quoted from F.N.Robinson ed. *The Complete Works of Geoffrey Chaucer*, 2nd edition, 1957.

7 See, for example, A.Brusendorff, *The Chaucer Tradition*, 1924, p.443; and J.L.Lowes, *PMLA* XX, 1905, p.753, note 4.

8 On the date of the poem see W.W.Skeat ed. *Chaucerian and other Pieces*, 1897, p.lviii; Brusendorff *op. cit.*, p.444; C.E.Ward, *MLN* XLIV, 1929, 225; Ethel Seaton, *Sir Richard Roos*, 1961, pp.91, 338, 390.

9 For descriptions see F.Madan, *Summary Catalogue of Western Manuscripts in the Bodleian Library*, Nos.3876, 2078, 3354, 10173.

10 See particularly R.H.Robbins, *PMLA* LXIX, 1954, 610-642.

11 Ethel Seaton, *op. cit.*, pp.105-106, thinks that the name "Gyl Astley 1460" might refer to an owner among the Astley family in Warwickshire.

12 A literary amateur, the patron of Gavin Douglas; see his *Aeneid* ed. J.Small, 1874, II, pp.5-6, IV, p.228

13 See Skeat, *op. cit.*, p.lvii; and E.Vollmer ed. *Das Mittelenglische Gedicht "The Boke of Cupide"*, 1898,

pp.9-16. But the figures given are based on my own investigations.

14 *op. cit.*, p.223, note 64.

15 E.Guest, *A History of English Rhythms*, 1882, p.649.

16 H.Chatelain, *Les Vers Français au XVe Siecle*, 1908, p.130.

17 Quoted by Janet M.Smith, *The French Background to Middle Scots Literature*, 1934, p.161.

18 *Chronicon Henrici Knighton*, ed. J.R.Lumby, RS 1889-1895, II 181; *Historia Anglicana*, ed. H.T.Riley, RS 1863-1864, II 159, 216; *Johannis de Trokelowe et Henrici de Blaneford Chronica et Annales*, ed. H.T. Riley, RS 1866, pp.290-291.

19 *Scottish Historical Review* XI, 55-92.

20 *Lancastrian Kings and Lollard Knights*, 1972, pp.139-226.

21 *Cal. Close Rolls, 1385-1389*, p.208; McFarlane, p.198.

22 McFarlane, pp.207-220.

23 H.O.Coxe, *Catologus Codicum MSS qui in Collegiis...
Oxoniensibus adservantur*, 1852, I, 28-29.

24 *op. cit.*, pp.200-201.

25 *The Middle English Translations of Robert Grosseteste's Château d'Amour*, 1967, p.123.

26 *TLS*, 8th February 1936, p.116.

27 For a critical summary of ideas about the authorship of *The Boke of Cupide* see my article in *Anglia* LXXXII, 1964, 137-149.

28 *Academy*, 1896, p.365.

29 *op. cit.*, p.630.

30 By Skeat, *Chaucerian and Other Pieces*, p.lix; Vollmer,

op. cit., p.59; Brusendorff, *op. cit.*, p.443; Ward, *op. cit.*, p.217.

[31] See, for example, Ethel Seaton, *op. cit.*, p.388.

[32] *Cal. Close Rolls, 1377-1381*, p.374.

[33] See J.Webb, *Archaeologia* XX, 1824, 320.

[34] For the will see N.H.Nicolas, *Testamenta Vetusta*, 1826, I, 109. For his relations with Chaucer and Graunson see H.Braddy, *Chaucer and the French Poet Graunson*, 1947, p.22. Deschamps wrote two ballades on d'Angle's death: see *Oeuvres, op. cit.*, III 320 (No. 495), IV 120 (No.661) and also IX 378.

[35] See *Oeuvres, op. cit.*, II 138, III 375; and G.L.Kittredge, *Modern Philology* I, 1903, 1-18.

[36] See particularly Edith Rickert, *Modern Philology* XI, 1913, 209-225.

[37] *Chroniques*, ed. K.de Lettenhove, 1876, particularly XV 157, 167.

[38] Now British Museum MS Royal 19 B XIII.

[39] See McFarlane, p.185.

[40] Edith Rickert, *Chaucer's World*, 1948, pp.404-407.

[41] *op. cit.*, p.184.

[42] The conclusions are based on the very full evidence provided by McFarlane, pp.230-232 (Appendix B).

[43] T.Rymer, *Foedera*, 1830, III part 2, 725.

[44] *op. cit.*, VII 456, 449.

[45] N.H.Nicolas, *The controversy between Sir Richard Scrope and Sir Robert Grosvenor*, 1832, II 437; Froissart, *Chroniques*, VII 879.

[46] McFarlane, p.179.

[47] *Enrolled Accounts* F. 2 Rich II A (quoted by Waugh, *op.cit.*).

48 *Cal. Pat. Rolls 1370-1374*, p.325.

49 *ibid.*, p.301.

50 *John of Gaunt's Register*, ed. S.Armitage-Smith, Camden Society, 3rd series XXI, II 191; *Rotuli Parliamentorum* II 326-327.

51 *Cal. Pat. Rolls, 1377-1381*, pp.71, 280; *Cal. Pat. Rolls, 1381-1385*, p.8.

52 *Cal. Pat. Rolls, 1377-1381*, p.627; *ibid., 1381-1385*, p.104.

53 *Rotuli Scotiae* II 75a; *Proceedings and Ordinances of the Privy Council*, I 8.

54 *Foedera* VII 466, 491, 513-514, 519.

55 *Exchequer Accounts*, K.R.Wardrobe 401-419 (quoted by Waugh, *op. cit.*).

56 *Proceedings and Ordinances of the Privy Council*, I 6-9.

57 *Cal. Pat. Rolls 1388-1392*, p.217.

58 *Polychronicon*, ed. J.R.Lumby, RS 1886, IX 234, 240.

59 *op. cit.*, XIV 287-288, 355-356.

60 *op. cit.*, IX 261-262.

A NOTE ON THE TEXTS

The text of *The Boke of Cupide* is taken from Bodleian
MS Fairfax 16 with variant readings from the other
authorities. The text of *The Two Ways* is taken from
University College Oxford MS 97 with variant readings
from British Museum MS Additional 22283.

Punctuation and capitalization are editorial as is
the lineation of the prose text, but the word-division
of the manuscripts has been followed except in cases
where obvious prefixes have been separated from the rest
of the word. The original paragraphing of the prose text
has been followed. Scribal contractions have been expanded without notice. Letters or words added by emenda-
tion have not been marked in the final text, but in all
cases where the final text differs from the copy text
the copy text reading has been noted among the variant
readings.

The variant readings intend to include all substan-
tive variations from the final text in all the authorities used. It has been the purpose to include all
variations of word order, all omissions of words and all
omissions or transpositions of lines. Spelling variants
are not recorded.

I

THE BOKE OF CUPIDE

The Boke of Cupide, God of Loue.

The god of love, a! benedicite,   (f.35v)
How myghty and how grete a lorde is he!
For he can make of lowe hertys hie,
And highe lowe, and like for to die
And herde hertis he can make fre.   5

And he can make, within a lytel stounde,
Of seke folke ful freshe, hool and sounde,
And of hoole he can make seke;
He can bynde and vnbynde eke,
What he wole haue bounde and vnbounde.   10

To telle his myght my wit may not suffice,
For he may do al that he can deuyse;
For he can make of wise folke ful nyse,
And in lyther folke dystroye vise,
And proude hertys he can make agryse.   15

Shortely, al that euere he wol he may,
Ayenst him ther dar no wight say nay;
For he can glade and greve whom him lyketh,

1. god] lorde S. / a] a a S.: ah Th.
3. lowe] low F. / hertys] herty F.
4. highe lowe] high hertis low F.B.: of hye lowe
   Ff.S.T.Th. / for to] to S.
5. herde] of hard S.
6. And] T.Th. *omit.*
7. ful] T.Th. *omit* / freshe] fresh F. / freshe hool]
   hoole fressh Ff.S.T.Th.
8. hoole] hale folk S.
9. He] And he S.
10. What] Quhom þat S.: That T.Th. / and] or Ff.T.Th.
12. and 13. T.Th. *transpose.*
12. can] wol Ff.T.Th.
14. in] into S.: T.Th. *omit.*/ dystroye] to destroien T.Th.
17. ther] Ff.T.Th. *omit.*
18. him] he Ff.

And who that he wol he laugheth or he siketh,
And most his myght he sheweth euer in May   20

ffor euery trewe, gentil herte fre
That with him is, or thinketh for to be,
Ayens May now shal haue somme steryng,
Other to ioy, or elles to morenynge,
In no seson so grette, as thynkes me.   25

ffor when they mowe her the briddes sing,
And see the floures and the leves spring,
That bringes in to hertis remembraunce
A maner ease, medled with grevaunce,
And lusty thoghtes ful of grete longynge.   30

And of that longynge cometh heuynesse,
And thereof groves ofte grete seknesse
And al for lak of that that they desyre;
And thus in May ben hertys set on fire,   (f.36r)
And so they brenne forthe in grete distresse.   35

19. he laugheth or he siketh] don him laugh or siketh
    F.B.: he laugethe or sigheth Ff.T.Th.: laughith or
    he sikith S.
20. he sheweth] schewith he S.: he shedeþ T.Th.
21. ffor] Fro Ff. / trewe] trew F. / herte] hert F.:
    hertes S. / fre] and free S.
22. is] ar S. / for to] to F.B.
24. Other] Or Ff.T.Th. / morenynge] some mornynge Ff.T.Th.
25. grette] mych T.Th.
26. when] then F. / mowe] mow F. / the] B.*omits.* /
    briddes] foulis S.
27. see the floures] þe floures se T.
28. bringes] burges F.
29. ease] case F.B.
32. ofte] oft F.: oft tyme S.
33. And al for lak] And for lak F.Ff.T.Th.: For lak B./
    that that] that F.B.Ff.: it þat S.
34. on] a Ff.S.
35. And so] So þat T.Th.

I speke this of felyng trewely,
For al thogh I be olde and vnlusty,
Yet haue I felt of that sekenes in May
Bothe hote and colde, an accesse euery day,
How sore ywis ther wot no wight but I.   40

I am so shaken with the feueres white,
Of al this May yet slept I but a lyte;
And also hit is vnlyke to me
That eny herte shulde slepy be,
In whom that love his firy dart wol smyte.   45

But as I lay this other nyght wakyng,
I thoght how louers had a tokenyng,
And among hem hit was a comvne tale
That hit wer good to her the nyghtyngale
Rather then the leude cukkow syng.   50

And then I thoght anon as hit was day,
I wolde goo somme whedir for to assay
Yf that I myght a nyghtyngale here,

36. speke this] speke all this S. / trewely] truly F.
37. For al thogh I] Thowgh I Ff.: If I T.Th.
38. haue I] I haue T.Th. / in May] thurgh may Ff.T.Th.:
    this may S.
39. an] one S.: and T.Th.
41. shaken] alayn F.B.
42. yet] ne Ff.: T.Th. *omit*. / slept] slepe S.T.Th.
43. is vnlyke to me] is vnlyke for to be F.B.: is not
    like to me Ff.T.Th.: naught likith vnto me S.
44. eny] my S. / herte] hert F. / slepy] asleping S.
46. But] And S.
48. was] is B.
50. leude] lowde Ff.
51. as] quhen S.
52. I] That I S. / for to] to T.Th.

For yet I non had herd of al this yere;
And hit was tho the thirde nyght of May.   55

And anon as I the day espied,
No lenger wolde I in my bed abyde;
But in to a wode that was fast by,
I went forthe allone priuely,
And helde my way don on a broke syde.   60

Til I come in to a launde of white and grene,
So feire oon had I neuere inne bene.
The grounde was grene, poudred with dayse,
The floures and the gras ilike hie,
Al grene and white was no thing elles sene.   65

Ther sat I dovne amonge the feire floures   (f.36v)
And sawe the briddes crepe out of her boures,
Ther as they had rested hem al nyght.

54. I non had herd] had y non herde Ff.S.Th.: herd I non
    T. / this] the Ff.: that S.Th.
55. tho] F.B. *omit.*
56. And anon] And than anon S.
58. in to] to Ff.: vnto T.Th. / that] Ff. *omits.*
59. forthe] me forth S. / priuely] boldly Ff.T.Th.
60. And helde my way] And helde the weye Ff.Th.: And
    held me þe wai T. / don on] doun by Ff.S.T.Th.
61. in to] til Ff.T.Th.: to S. / white and grene] white
    and of grene Ff.
62. oon] ne S. / inne] in F.
63.and 64. B. *transposes.*
64. gras] grenes Ff.T.: greses S.: greves Th. / ilike
    hie] al ilike hie F.B.: lyke hye Ff.T.Th.
65. Al grene] Rede grene S.
67. And] I S. / the] thee F. / crepe] trippe Ff.T.Th.:
    flee S.
68. had rested hem] rested han Ff.: thame rested S.:
    rested hem T.Th. / al nyght] all the nyght Ff.T.Th.:
    all that nyght S.

38

They were so ioyful of the dayes lyght,
That they began of May to don her houres.   70

They coude that seruise alle bye rote.
Ther was mony a lovely note:
Somme songe loude, as they hadde playned,
And somme in other maner voys yfeyned,
And somme al out, with al the fulle throte.   75

They pruned hem, and made hem ryght gay,
And davnseden, and lepten on the spray,
And euermore two and two in fere,
Ryght so as they had chosen hem to yere
In Marche, vponn Seynt Valentynes day.   80

And the ryver that I sat vpon,
Hit made such a noyse as hit ronne,
Acordaunt to the foules ermonye.

70. That] Ff.T.Th. *omit.* / of] on S. / to don her
    houres] ben ther houres F.B.: vse their houris S.:
    for to don houres T.Th.
71. that seruise alle] nat seruice al Ff.T.: wele all
    that service S.
72. lovely note] lusty strange note S.
73. loude] lowe Ff.S. / hadde] had F. / pleyned]
    compleyned S.
74. yfeyned] enfeyned S.
75. somme al out] som song out S. / al the fulle] a
    lowde F.B.: all full S.
76. made hem] made hym Ff. / ryght] wonder S. / gay] gay
    gay Ff.
77. davnseden] dansen S. / and] and thei S. / lepten]
    lepen S.T.
79. they] the Ff. / to] that Ff.
80. Marche] fevirȝere T.Th.
81. And the] And eke the S. / vpon] vpon than S.
83. Acordaunt] According S. / to] wyth Ff.T.Th. / foules]
    bryddes Ff.S.T.Th.

Me thoght hit was the beste melodye
That myghte ben yherd of eny mon.   85

And for delyte therof, I note ner how,
I fel in such a slombre and a swowe—
Not al on slepe, ne fully wakynge—
And in that swowe me thoght I herde singe
That sory bridde, the lewede cukkowe.   90

And that was on a tre ryght faste bye,
But who was then euel apayed but I.
"Now God," quod I, "that died vponn the croise,
Yive sorrowe on the, and on thy foule voyse,
For lytel ioy haue I now of thy crie."   95

And as I with the cukkow thus gan chide,
I herde, in the next busshe me beside,

84. beste] best F.
85. myghte] myght F. / ben yherd] be herd F. / mon]
    man F.: lifand man S.
86. therof] F.B.T.Th. *omit.* / note] woote Ff.T.Th. / ner]
    neuer Ff.S.T.Th.
87. in such] in to S. / swowe] slow B.S.
88. on slepe] a slepe T. / ne] nor S. / full wakynge]
    fully all waking S.
89. swowe] slowe S. / thoght I] thoght þat I S.:
    þouȝ I T.
90. That] The S.T.Th. / lewede] lewde F.: lowde Ff.
91. on] in S. / faste] fast F. / ryght faste bye] fast
    me by S.
92. apayed] payde Ff.
93. vponn] on Ff.S.T.Th.
94. foule] lewde T.Th.
96. as] so F. / thus gan chide] gan chide F.B.: now gan
    chyde Ff.: gan to chide S.
97. busshe] busshes F.: beugh S. / me] Ff.S.T.Th. *omit.*

40

A nyghtyngale so lustely singe,
That with her clere woys she made rynge
Thro out al the grene wode wide.   (f.37r) 100

"A! good nyghtyngale," quod I then,
"A lytell hast thou be to longe hen,
For her hath be the lewede cukkow,
And songen songes rather then hast thou.
I prey to God that euel fire him brenne."   105

But now I wil yow tel a wonder thinge;
As longe as I lay in that swonynge,
Me thoght I wist al that the briddes ment,
And what they seyde, and what was her entent,
And of her speche I had good knovynge.   110

And then herd I the nyghtyngale sey,
"Now, good cukkow, go somme where thy wey,
And let vs that can synge duelle here;
For euery wight escheweth the to here,
Thy songes be so elynge, in gode fey."   115

 98. so lustely singe] full lustely ysing S.
100. Thro out] Thurghe Ff.T.Th. / grene wode] grenes of
      the wode Ff.: grene woddis S.
103. lewede] lewde F.: lowde Ff.T.
104. hast] F.B. *omit*.
105. that] T.Th. *omit*. / him] hir S.Th.
107. As] Als S. / swonynge] slombering S.
108. al that] what T.Th.
110. I had good] had I grete S.
111. And then herd I] I herd aӡeyne S.: And þere herd
      I T.: There herde I Th.
112. thy wey] away Ff.T.Th.
113. synge] syng F. / duelle] duel F. / here] he T.
115. Thy] The Ff. / elynge] lewed S.

41

"What!" quoth he, "what may the eyle now?
Hit thynkes me I syng as wel as thow;
For my songe is bothe trewe and pleyn,
Al thogh I can not breke hit so in veyne,
As thou dost in thy throte, I wote ner how.   120

And euery wight may vnderstonde me,
But, nyghtyngale, so may they not the,
For thou has mony a nyse, queynte crie.
I haue herd the seye 'ocy! ocy!'
Who myght wete what that shulde be?"   125

"O fole," quoth she, "wost thou not what that is?
When that I sey 'ocy! ocy!' iwisse,
Then mene I that I wolde wonder fayne
That alle tho wer shamefully slayne,
That menen oght ayen love amys.   130

116. What quoth] Quhat bird quod S. / he] she F.B.
117. Hit] Me S. / me] þat S.
118. bothe] both F. / and pleyn] and also pleyne S.
119. Al thogh] And þouȝ T.Th. / breke hit] crake Ff.:
     crekill S.T.Th.
120. ner] neuer Ff.S.Th.: not T.
121. vnderstonde] vnderstond F.
122. not the] not do the Ff.S.T.Th.
123. nyse] F.B.S. *omit.* / queynte] queynt F.: queynt
     feyned S.
124. haue herd the] the haue herde Ff.: the haue herd
     the S.: haue þe herd T.Th. / seye] sing S.
125. Who] Howe Ff.T.Th.: Bot quho S. / wete] y knowe
     Ff.T.Th.: vnderstand S. / shulde] shuld F.:
     myght S.
126. O] A Ff.T.: Ah Th. / she] he S. / that] it Ff.T.Th.
127. that] than Ff. / sey] sing S.
128. mene I that] mene I thus þat S.
129. alle] al F. / tho] they Ff.T.Th.

42

And also, I wold alle tho were dede,
That thenke not her lyve in love to lede,   (f.37v)
For who that wol the god of love not serve,
I dar wel say he is worthy for to sterve,
And for that skille 'ocy! ocy!' I grede."   135

"Ey!" quoth the cukkow, "this is a queynt lawe,
That eyther shal I love or elles be slawe.
But I forsake al suche companye,
ffor myn entent is neyther for to dye,
Ne, while I lyve, in loves yoke to drawe.   140

ffor louers be the folke that lyven on lyve,
That most disese han, and most vnthrive,
And most enduren sorowe, wo and care,
And, at the last, failen of her welfaire.
What nedith hit ayens trweth to strive?"   145

131. also] al they S. / alle tho] al tho F.: that all
     tho Ff.T.Th.: also S. / were dede] had the dede
     Ff.T.Th.
132. thenke] thenk F. / her lyve in love] in loue her life T.Th.
133. who that] quhoso S.: who so that Th. / wol the god
     of love not] wol not the god of loue Ff.T.Th.
134. he] S. *omits*. / is] ar S. / for to] to Ff.T.Th.
135. grede] crede F.: cryed S.
136. this is] ywis this is F.B.
137. eyther shal I] euery wight shall Ff.S.T.Th. / elles
     be slawe] bene to drawe Ff.T.Th.
139. neyther] not Ff.T.Th. / for to] F. *omits*.
140. Ne while] Ne neuer whiles Ff.T.Th.: Nor quhill S.
     / in] on T.Th. / yoke] loke F.
141. lyven] bene Ff.S.T.Th. / on] of F.
142. han] suffren S. / vnthrive] and vnthrive F.
144. at the last] lest Ff.T.Th.: alderlaste haue S.
     / failen] feelen Ff.T.Th.: felyng S. / her]
     Ff.S.T.Th. *omit*.
145. nedith] nede is Ff.

43

"What!" quoth she, "thou art out of thy mynde.
How maist thou in thy cherles herte fynde
To speke of loves seruauntes in this wyse?
For in this worlde is noon so good seruise
To euery wight that gentil ys of kynde.   150

ffor therof truly cometh al goodnesse,
Al honour and al gentilnesse,
Worship, ese, and al hertys lust,
Perfyt ioy and ful ensured trust,
Iolite, plesaunce and freshenesse,   155

Lovelyhed and trewe companye,
Semelyhed, largesse and curtesie,
Drede of shame and forto don amys;
ffor he that truly loues seruaunt ys,
Wer lother to be schamed then to dye.   160

146. What] Quhat brid S.
147. maist] myght Ff.T.Th. / cherles] cherlnesse Ff.Th.:
     cherlich S.: clerenes T. / herte] hert F.:
     Ff.T.Th. *omit*.
148. seruauntes] seruant Ff.
149. worlde] word T.
151. truly cometh] cumyth trewely S. / goodnesse]
     gladnesse Ff.
152. Al honour] Honestee estate S.
153. Worship ese] Worship and es S. / and al] and F.B.
     / hertys] hurtys F.
154. ensured] assured Ff.S.T.Th. / trust] liste Ff.
155. and] and eke S.
156.and 157. T.Th. *transpose the second halves*.
156. trewe] trew F.
157. largesse] largenesse F.
158. B. *omits but includes after 160 with a correction
     mark*.
158. and] Ff.T.Th. *omit*. / forto] fo to Ff.
160. to be] be Ff.T.Th. / then to] then for to B.: then
     do Ff.

And that ys sothe, alle that I sey.
In that beleve I wol bothe lyve and dye,
And, cukkow, so rede I that thou do iwis."
"Ye then," quoth he, "God let me neuer haue blis,
If euere I to thy counseyl obey.   (f.38r) 165

Nyghtyngale, thou spekest wonder faire,
But, for al that, the sothe is the contreyre.
For loving is in yonge folke but rage,
And in olde hit is a grete dotage,
Who most hit vseth, most he shal apeyre.   170

For ther of cometh disese and heuynesse,
Sorow and care and mony a grete seknesse,

161. that ys] that it be S.: þat þis is T.Th. / alle
     that] of al that F.: that Ff.T.Th.: al þat euer S.
162. bothe] T.Th.*omit.*
163. rede I that thou] rede I the that thou F.B.: I rede
     thou Ff.: I rede þat thou T.Th.
164. Ye] Ff.T.Th. *omit.* / then] God S. / he] she F.B.
     / God] S.T.Th. *omit.*
165. to] vnto T.Th. / thy] that Ff.T.Th.
167. the sothe is the] ys the soth Ff.T.Th.: full sooth
     is the S.
168. loving] loue T.Th. / is in yonge folke] in yong
     folke is F. / but rage] bot a rage S.
169. olde] old folk S.T.Th. / hit is] S.T.Th. *omit.* / a
     grete] a full grete S.
170. most he shal] shall most Ff.: most it schall S.:
     most shal T.Th. / apeyre] en pair Ff.S.T.Th.
171. disese and] mony an F.B.
172. Sorow] So sorowe Th. / and mony] with many S. /
     grete] F.B. *omit.*

45

Dispite, debate, angre and envye,
Repreve and shame, vntrust and ielosye,
Pride and myschefe, pouert and wodenesse.   175

What! louyng is an office of dispaire,
And oon thing is ther in that ys not faire;
For who that geteth of love a lytil blysse,
But if he be alway ther by ywysse,
He may ful sone of age haue his eire.   180

And therfor, nyghtyngale, holde the nye,
For leve me wel, for al thy lovde crie,
Yf thou be fer or longe fro thi make,
Thou shalt be as other that be forsake,
And then shalt thou hoten as do I."   185

"ffye!" quoth she, "on thi name and on the.
The god of love ne let the neuere ythe!

174. Repreve] Disproue Ff.: Deprauyng T.Th. / and shame]
     shame T.Th. / vntrust] to trust F.
175. Pride and] Pride B.Ff.T.Th.
176. What] Ff.T.Th. *omit.*
178. Who that] quhoso S.
179. if] F.B. *omit.* / alway ther by] therby alwey S.:
     alwai þer with T.Th.
180. may ful sone of age haue] most of age soon haue S.
     / his] one S. / eire] crie F.B.: aire S.
181. therefor nyghtyngale] nyghtingale therfor Ff.T.Th.:
     nyghtyngale therof S.
182. leve me wel] love wole S. / lovde] queynt Ff.S.T.Th.
183. thou be fer or longe] thou fer of long be F.: thou
     fer or long be B.: thou be long and fer S.
184. Thou] Then B. / as other] as one othir S.
185. shalt thou hoten] thu shalt hoten Ff.T.Th.: thou
     shalt haten love S. / do I] as wele as I S.: I do T.
186. ffye] Now fy S. / on thi] upon thy S. / and on]
     and S.
187. ne] F.B. *omit.*: now S.

46

For thou art wors a thousand folde then wode,
For mony oon is ful worthie and ful good,
That had be noght ne had love ybe.   190

ffor love his seruant euermore amendeth,
And fro al euel tachches him defendeth,
And maketh him to brenne as eny fire,
In trouthe and in worschipful desire,
And whom him likes, ioy ynogh him sendeth."   195

"Ye, nyghtyngale," he seyde, "holde the stille!
ffor love hath no reson but his wille;   (f.38v)
For ofte sithe vntrew folke he esith,
And trewe folke so bittirly displesith,
That for defaute of grace hee let hem spille.   200

189. mony oon is] mony is F.B.: mony one ar S.
190. be noght] not ben S.
191. love his seruant euermore] euermore loues seruauntez
     Ff.: love his seruandis euermore S.: euermore loue
     his seruantis T.Th.
192. euel] F.B. *omit*. / tachches] scathis S. / him] hem
     Ff.S.T.Th.
193. him] hem Ff.S.T.Th. / to brenne] be brynnyng S. /
     as] ryght as Ff.T.: right in Th. / eny] Ff. *omits*.:
     a S.T.Th.
194. and in] honour and S. / worschipful] worschip to S.
195. whom] when Ff.T.Th. / him likes] hem likeþ T.Th. /
     ioy] I seye S. / him sendeth] hem sendith Ff.T.Th.:
     he sendith S.
196. Ye] Thou Ff.S.T.Th. / holde the] now hold the S.:
     be Th.
197. his] it is T.Th.
198. sithe] tymes S.: tyme T.Th. / vntrew] full vntrewe
     Ff.
199. trewe] trew F. / so] full S. / bittirly displesith]
     bitterly he displesith Ff.T.Th.
200. That] And F.B. / grace] corage Th.

With such a lorde wolde I neuer be,
For he is blynde and may not se.
And when he lyeth he not, ne when he fayleth;
In this court ful selde trouthe avayleth,
So dyuerse and so wilful ys he."   205

Then toke I of the nyghtyngale kepe.
She kest a sighe out of her herte depe,
And seyde, "Alas, that euer I was bore!
I can for tene sey not oon worde more."
And ryght with that she brast on forto wepe.   210

"Alas!" quoth she, "my hert wol to breke,
To here thus this false bridde to speke
Of loue, and of his worshipful seruyse.
Now, god of love, thou helpe me in summe wise,
That I may on this cukkow ben awreke."   215

Me thoghte then that I stert vp anone,
And to the broke I ran and gatte a stone,

201.to 205. T.Th. *omit.*
202. blynde and] blynd alweye and S. / not] nothyng Ff.
203. And] S. *omits.* / when] whom Ff.S. / lyeth] hit Ff.:
     hurtith S. / ne when] or whom Ff.: ne quhom S. /
     fayleth] helith S.
204. In] And in Ff.: Into S. / this] his Ff.S.
207. She] And she Ff.: Hou she T.Th. / herte] hert F.:
     Ff.T.Th. *omit.*
208. seyde] sey Ff. / Alas] Allone S. / euer I] I euer F.B.
209. I can] And gan S. / sey not] nouȝ sey T.Th.
210. that] þat word Th. / on] oute Ff.T.Th.: anon S. /
     forto] to S.Th.
212. here] her F. / false] fals F.: leude Th. / to]
     S.T.Th. *omit.*
214. thou] S. *omits.* / helpe me] me help S. / in] into S.
216. thoghte] thoght F. / that] Ff.T.Th. *omit.* / I] he Th.
     / vp] out F.B.
217.to 219. T.Th. *omit.*

48

And at the cukkow hertely I cast,
And he for drede flyed awey ful fast,
And glad was I when that he was agone.   220

And euermore the cukkow as he fley,
He seyde, "Farewel, farewel, papyngay."
As thogh he had scorned, thoghte me.
But ay I hunted him fro tre to tre,
Till he was fer al out of syght away.   225

And then come the nyghtyngale to me
And seyde, "Frende, for soth I thanke the,
That thou hast lyked me thus to rescowe,
And oon avowe to love I avowe,
That al this May I wol thy singer be."   (f.39r) 230

I thanked her, and was ryght wel apayed.
"Yee," quoth she, "and be thou not amayed

218. at] to Ff. / hertely] hertly F.: hardily S. / I] Ff.
     omits.
219. he for drede] for drede he Ff.: he for drede gan S.
220. when] T.Th. *omit*. / agone] gone F.
222. He] T.Th. *omit*.
223. thoghte me] thoght me F.: as thoght me S.: me
     aloone T.Th.
224.and 225. T.Th. *omit*.
224. fro tre to tre] fro the tre Ff.
225. Till] Quhill S. / al out of syght] oute of syght Ff.:
     fro sight out S.
226. the] this S. / to] vnto S.
228. thou hast lyked] the hath lyked Ff. / thus] Ff.T.Th.
     omit.: for S.
229. oon avowe] riȝt anon S. / I avowe] I wol avowe Ff.:
     I wole allowe S.: make I now T.Th.
230. That] And T.Th. / wol] shall S.
231. ryght] full S.
232. and] ne S. / amayed] dismaied T.Th.

Thogh thou haue herde the cukkow er then me;
For, if I lyve, hit shal amended be
The nexte May, yf I be not affrayed.   235

And oon thing I wol rede the also:
Ne leve not the cukkow, loves fo,
For al that he hath seyde is strong lesing."
"Nay," quoth I, "ther shal no thing me bring
Fro love, and yet he doth me mekil wo."   240

"Yee, vse thou," quoth she, this medecyne,
Euery day this May, er that thou dyne:
Goo loke vpon the fresshe flour daysye,
And thogh thou be for wo in poynt to dye,
That shal ful gretly lyssen the of thy pyne.   245

And loke alwey that thou be good and trewe,
And I wol singe oon of thy songes newe.

233. the cukkow] the fals cukkow S. / er then me] greue
      me S.: syng erst þan me T.
235. The] This S. / nexte] next F. / not] nought S.
236. I wol] wole I S. / rede the also] rede the do also S.
237. leve not] love not F.B.: loue thou nat Ff.T.Th.:
      leue thou not S. / loves fo] the louce foo Ff.: ne
      his louys foo T.Th.
238. al] that S.
239. Nay] Nay nay S. / ther] ther to T.Th. / no thing]
      noman T.
240. Fro] For Ff.T.Th. / yet he doth] if haþ do T.Th. /
      mekil] mochel Ff.: moche S.T.Th.
241. vse thou] vse Ff.T.Th.: thou shalt vse S.
242. that] Ff.T.Th. *omit.*
243. Goo] To S. / fresshe] fressh F. / flour] Ff.T.Th.
      omit. / daysye] the daysye F.B.
245. That] Thal Ff. / gretly] mekle S. / lyssen the] the
      lyssen F.B.: lessen S. / of] T.Th. *omit.*
246.to end. *Lost in* S.
247. thy] my Ff.: þe T.Th.

For love of the, as loude as I may crie."
And then she began this songe ful hye,
"I shrewe hem al that be to love vntrewe."   250

And when she had songen hit to the ende,
"Now fairewel," quoth she, "for I most wende.
And, god of love, that can ryght wel and may,
As mekil ioy sende yow this day,
As euer yet he eny lover sende!"   255

Thus toke the nyghtyngal her leve of me.
I prey to God he alwey with her be,
And ioy of love he sende her euer more,
And shilde vs fro the cukkow and his lore,
For ther is non so fals a brid as he.   260

fforthe she fley, the gentil nyghtyngale,
To al the briddes that werne in the wale,   (f.39v)
And gat hem all in to a place yn fere,
And besoght hem that they wolde here
Her dysese, and thus began her tale: 265

"Yee knowe wel, hit is not fro yow hidde,
How that the cukkow and y fast haue chidde

248. may] kan Ff.
250. hem al] all hem T.Th. / to] of Ff.T.Th.
251. hit to] hit out to F.B.
254. sende] send F. / yow] the Ff.T.Th. / day] may Ff.
255. euer] eny T.Th. / he eny lover] louer he euer T.Th.
256. toke] takyght Ff.T.Th.
257. he] Ff.T.Th. *omit*. / with] whele Ff.
258. he] Ff. *omits*.
260. non] not T.Th. / as he] as is he T.
262. the] that Ff.T.Th. / wale] dale Ff.T.Th.
266. Yee knowe wel] Ye wyten wel for Ff.: The cukku wel
     T.Th. / is not fro yow hidde] may not be yhydde Ff.:
     is not for to hide T.Th.
267. that] Ff.T.Th. *omit*. / fast] F.B. *omit*.

51

Euer sithe hit was dayes lyght.
I prey yow alle that ye do me ryght
Of that foule, fals, vnkynde bridde."   270

Then spake oon brid for alle by assent:
"This mater asketh good avysement,
ffor we be fewe briddes her in fere,
And soth hit is the cukkow is not here,
And therfore we wol haue a parlement.   275

And ther at shal the egle be our lorde,
And other perys that ben of recorde,
And the cukkow shal be after sent,
And ther shal be yeven the iugement,
Or elles we shul make summe acorde.   280

And this shal be, withouten any nay,
The morowe of Seynt Valentynes day,
Vnder the maple that is feire and grene,
Before the chambre wyndow of the Quene
At Wodestok, vpon the grene lay."   285

268. Euer] Er Ff.
269. alle] al F.
271. oon] a Ff. / alle] al F. / by assent] by oune
        assent Ff.T.Th.
273. fewe] Th. *omits.*
276. shal the egle be] shal be the egle F.B.
277. of recorde] of o record Ff.
279. And] Ff.T.Th. *omit.*
280. make] fynalli make T.Th. / summe] Ff.T.Th. *omit.*
281. any] Ff.T.Th. *omit.* / nay] may T.
282. of] after Ff.T.Th.
283. the] a Ff.T.Th.
285. grene] grete Ff.

She thanketh hem and then her leve toke,
And fleye in to an hawthorn by the broke,
And ther she sate and songe vpon the tre:
"Terme of lyve, love hath withholde me"
So lovde, that with that songe I awoke.   290

Explicit liber Cupidinis.

286. thanketh] thanked T.Th. / and] Ff. *omits*. / then]
     the F.
287. fleye] T.Th. *omit*. / hawthorn] hawthornes F. / the]
     þat T.
288. the] a Ff.: þat T.Th.
290. with that songe I] I wyth that song Ff.T.Th. /
     awoke] began awake Ff.

II

THE TWO WAYS

[*f114r*] This tretis next folewynge maade Sir Johan Clanevowe,
knyȝt, þe laste viage þat he maade ouer the greete
see in whiche he dyede, of whos soul Ihesu haue
mercy. Amen.

The gospel telleþ þat in a tyme whanne oure lord   5
Ihesu Crist was heere vpon eerthe a man com to hym
and askede hym ȝef þat fewe men shulden be saaued.
And Crist answerede and seyde, "The ȝaate is wyde
and þe way is brood þat leedeþ to los and manye goon
in þat wey, and how streit is þe ȝaate and þe weye   10
nargh þat leedeth to þe lyf and few fynden þat
wey." [*f114v*] By thise woordis of Crist we mown vndirstoonde
þat þe way þat leedeþ to þe peyne of helle is a
brood wey and þat þe wey þat leedeþ to þe blisse
of heuene is a nargh wey. ffor Crist cleepeþ þe   15
peyne of helle los and þe blisse of heuene lyf.
And, þerfore, it weer ful good þat we shoopen vs for
to eschewe þat broode way and for to goo in that
nargh wey, ffor we been euery day goyng ful faste
towardis anoþer place and we wyten neuere how soone   20
we shuln out of þis world. And whanne we shuln passe
hennes who þat is þat tyme founden in þat broode wey
he shal withouten let to þe peyne of helle, and who þat
is þat tyme founden in þe nargh wey he shal withouten
let to þe blisse of heuene. And þat blisse is so greet   25
þat noon eye hath seyn, ne eere yherd, ne it hath not
comen into mannes herte þe ioye þat God haþ ordeyned
for hem þat louen hym and shuln come þider. And þat
ioye is not lich þe ioye of þis world, ffor al þe ioye
of þis world is passynge, and soone ydoon, and foule   30
ymedled with dreede and with manye ooþer diseesis
and trauailles. But þe ioye of heuene is moore and
moore, and noo dreede, ne trauail, ne diseeses
þereinne, ne lakkyng of noo þing þat herte may desire;
and þerto it lasteþ withouten eende. And, þerfore, wel   35
is hym þat is founden in þat nargh wey whan he
passeþ out of þis world, for he shal eueremoore dwelle
with God in euere lastynge blisse. And woo is hym
þat is founden in þe broode wey whanne he shal

40 passe out of þis world, for he shal to þe paynes
of helle. And þat payne is vnlyche any payne of
þis worlde, ffor iche payne or turment of þis world
mot haaue an eende oþer by deeþ or by sum oother
wey. But þe payne of helle is grettere þan any
45 herte kan þinke and shal neuere haaue eende, but
it shal alwey bee moore and moore. And he þat is
þere shal neuere dyen but euere lyuen among the
feendis in derknesse and in turment withouten eende.
And, þerfore, crie we to oure lord God, and preye we
50 hym of his eendeles mercy þat he teeche vs his
nargh wey, and ȝeue vs grace to leeue þe brood wey. But
þanne muste we bee meeke and crie to hym with meeke
herte, ffor þe prophete seith þat God shal teechen hem
þat been meeke hise weyes. And þerfore meekely crie we
55 to hym with þe prophete þat seith, "Lord, shewe me þi
weyes and teeche me thi styes." But þanne ȝef God of
his goodnesse teecheþ vs hise weyes and we vnkyndely
leeuen hise weyes and goon oothere weyes, we been muchel
to blaame and worthi greete penaunce. And moor harme
60 is manye [f115r] doon soo, ffor þouȝ þei knowen þe weyes of
God ȝet þei leeuen hem and goon þe weyes of þe feend
for lust of here flesshe or lykynge of þe world. And,
sikerly, þei been grettere fooles þan þei þat woln not
ȝeuen here babelis for alle þe kynges tresour. ffor a
65 babel is an instrument þat is maad of þing þat is
litel worth, and with þat a fool beeteþ ooþere men,
and ofte tymes oothere men beeten hym þerwith aȝen,
so þat he smyteþ and is smyten aȝen therwith, and it
serueth of not elles. And þat a fool wol alwey
70 haaue neiȝ hym and he wol leeue it for noo thyng.
And whanne þat a fool loueþ so wel his babel, þat,
men seyn, is þe preeue of a naturel fool. But ȝet
been þei moore fooles preued þat woln not leeue here
soory lustes þat been worse þan babelis, with þe whiche
75 lustes þei greeuen ofte oothere folke and also þei
been greued hem self. And ȝet þei woln not ȝeuen
hem for alle þe kynges tresour of heuene. And, þerfore,
in hem men mowen wel knowe þat þe woord of Crist

58

is verified þat seith þus, "The wysdoom of þis world
is folie byfore God." Þerfore, for þe loue of God   80
and of oure owene soules vse we not þat folie.
But whanne þat we knowen þe weyes of God, preye
we hertely to hym þat he ȝeue vs grace to hoolden
vs stedefastly in hem. And crie we ȝet aȝen to
hym with þe prophete þat seith, "Lord, maak   85
parfit myne outgoyngges in thi paþes so þat my
steppes been not meeued." And ȝef þat we been
besy oure self and preyen God mekly þat he helpe
vs, þanne shuln we lerne hise weyes and goon in
hem, and haaue þe blissyng þat Dauid spekeþ of   90
in þe sauter þere as he seith, "Blissed been all þoo
þat dreeden oure Lord and þat walken in hise weyes."
þat is to seye, blissed been alle þo þat goon in at
þe streite ȝaate and woln walke in the narugh wey.
For þis forseide nargh wey is þe kepyng of   95
Goddis commaundementȝ, and þat we mowen see and
knowe by þe woordis of Crist þat seide to oon þat
askede hym what he shulde doo to haue euerelastyng
lyf. And Crist answerde to hym, "Ȝef þu wolt entre
euerelastyng lyf keepe þe commaundementȝ." And by   100
þoo woordis and by manye oothere þat been in hooly
writ we mown wel knowen þat þer nys noon oothere
wey to heuene but by keepyng of Goddis hestes, so
þat þe hestes of God is the nargh wey þat leedeþ
to heuene. And þe strayte ȝaate is þe dreede of   105
God þoruȝ þe whiche dreede we shuln leeue oure
euele lustes. And þat we mowne wel knowe [f115v] by hooly
writ þat seith, "The dreede of God is þe bigynnyng
of wisdoom." And þere is no þing þat we mowne doo
of wysdom but þat þat leedeþ vs toward þe blisse   110
of heuene. And þanne is þe dreede of God þe
bigynnynge of þe narugh wey þat leedeþ to heuene
ward. And for it is þe bigynnyng and þe entree
of þat wey it is cleeped þe ȝaate. And þus we
mown see by resoun þat þe keepyng of Goddis   115
hestes is þe nargh wey þat leedeþ to lyf, and þe
dreede of God is þe streit ȝaate of þat wey. And

riȝt so in þe contrarie wyse þe breekyng of Goddis
hestes is þe broode wey þat leedeþ to þe peyne of
120 helle, ffor as þe prophete seith to God þat þei been
acursed þat bowen awey fro þe commaundementȝ of God.
And þe wyte ȝaate of þat broode wey is reechelesshipe
of þe keepyng of Goddis hestes, þoruȝ þe whiche
we folewen oure yuele lustes and so þoruȝ þat we
125 fallen into þe broode wey of helle. Fro þe whiche
God of his eendeles mercy keepe vs, and ȝeue vs
grace to goo in at þe streite ȝaate and hoolde
vs in þe nargh wey til þat it bee his wille to
taake vs in to þe lyf þat þat wey leedeth to.
130 And, sikerly, ȝef we been wyse we shuln crie nyȝt
and day to God þat he graunte vs þat. And truste
we fully in hym þat he wole graunten vs alle þat
good is for vs so þat we preyen hym with a trewe
herte. And, þerfore, goo we in to þe streyte ȝaate,
135 þat is to seye, dreede we oure lord God, for he
is þe bigynnyng of wisdom. And, sikerly, we
aughte weel to dreeden hym soore, for we haue no
beyng, ne lyf, ne weele, ne wyt, but oonly of hym
and by hym. And whanne þat hym lyketh he may
140 benymen vs þat. And also he is, and shal bee,
oure iuge. And he wot al þat we doon or haan
ydoon, and we mown nowher flee from his doom
for he is oueral and alle myȝty. And also
we been synful and synne muste neede bee punyssched
145 in this world or in anoother. And oure lord God þouȝ
he bee ful of mercy ȝet he is ful of riȝtwisnesse,
and, þerfore, dreede we hym ouer alle thyng. And
þat shal maaken vs to leeue oure ydel doynges and
yuele lustes the whiche we mown doo awey to greet
150 profit of oure self ȝef þat we woln marchaundise wysily.
ffor þei þat been holden wyse marchauntȝ in þis
world, þouȝ þei louen money neuer so wel, what tyme
þat any of hem seeþ þat he may with puttyng out of
twenty pounde wynne an hundrede pounde he is faynere
155 to putte forþ þoo twenty pound þanne he wolde bee to
drawe to hym fourty of fifty [f116r] pound. And also ȝef a

60

marchaunt woot þat he may with twenty pound or
ȝritty keepe hym fro þe harme of an hundred or twoo
hundred pound he is gladder to do out twenty or þritty
pound for þat cause þanne þat he wolde freely wynne   160
fifty pound or sixty. Trewely, muche moore shulde we
bee glad to doo awey oure yuel lustes and oure yuel
deedes, ffor with doyng awey of hem we mown withouten
any let wynne þe blisse of heuene and keepen vs fro þe
peyne of helle. And ȝef we doon thus we been   165
wyse marchauntȝ, and ȝef we doo not þus we been
foolys, thouȝ we geeten vs neuere so muche
worsshipe, and eese, or richesse of this world.
     But whanne þat oure lord Ihesu Crist spak of
thise forseyde weyes he bad hem þat þei shulden stryue   170
for to goo in by þe nargh and þe streyte ȝaate. And,
forsooth, so moote we doo ȝef þat we wolen go þerin,
ffor we han ȝre stronge enemys þat woln not by her
wille leten vs come þerin withouten greet stryf: þat
oon is þe feend; þat oother is þe world: þe ȝridde is   175
oure flesshe. Thise ȝree enemys been alwey abouten
for to leeden vs by þe wyde ȝaate into þe broode
wey of helle, and for to lette vs for to goo by þe
streite ȝaate in to þe nargh wey of heuene.
The feend is euere besy to letten vs with falsheed   180
and with wyles; oure flesshe is besy to letten vs
with his foule lykerousnesse and freelte; and þe
world is besy to letten vs with folye and vanite.
And þis is a ful hard werre. But, naþelees, we
mown wel taken ensaumple of þe seintes in heuene   185
þat been ypassed by þe narugh wey to þe blisse
of heuene maugree þise forseyde enemyes. And
also þei haan left here woord and her teechyng
to vs how þat we schuln come þider after hem
and withstoonde oure enemys, as þei deden, ȝef   190
þat we woln. And, þerfore, it is greete schame
to vs and eendelees harme also but ȝef we holden

160 þanne] U *omits*.

61

þe wey after þoo seyntes, ffor, with þe grace of
God, as wel mowe we goo þat wey, ʒef þat we
195 woln, as þei deden. ffor of þoo seyntes þeere
weeren summe oolde men and oolde wommen in
feblesse of here bodies, and summe ʒonge children,
and summe tendre maydenes, and summe weeren
strong folke of here bodies booþ men and wommen,
200 and summe riche, and summe poore. And of alle
þise forseide condiciouns of poeple þei woolden leeue
here lustes in þis worlde for to goo þoruʒ þe straite
ʒaate, ande, þerfore, þei been now in blisse and muchel
honoured booþe [*f116v*] in heuene and in eerthe. And riʒt
205 so mown we doo ʒef þat we woln loue and dreede
oure God and not bee recchelees of hym. ffor þe
wyse man seith that iche man schulde bowe awey
from yuel by dreede of God. And also þe prophet
seith that God is neiʒ to hem þat dreeden hym.
210   But, as it is seid heere bifore, the feend
wole letten vs al þat he may for to dreede God.
ffor he wole putte to vs þat it is noo neede to vs for
to dreede God so soore, ffor God is ful of mercy,
and with þe leeste crieng of mercy þat we konne
215 crie he wol forʒeuen vs. And ʒef we been shapen
to lyue loong tyme we mown wel vsen oure eeses
and oure lustes til þat we been neiʒ oure eende,
and þanne mown we crie mercy and haue
forʒeuenesse, and so we mown booþe haue oure
220 lustes in þis worlde and eek in heuene. And also
he seiþ ʒef þat þere bee heuene and helle as men
speketh of but þerof noo man woot and þerfore
of þis world taake we þat we mown, for þerof we
been syker. And oure flesshe wole putte to vs þat
225 he may not suffre for tendre, and þat he mot needes
faillen or elles he mot haaue hise lustes, and þat
lustes and eeses been ordeyned for þat he shulde
vse hem, and þat he may not bee merie withouten
hem, and þat he hadde leuere bee deed þan to
230 forberen hem. And þus wol þe flesshe gruchen.
Ande þe world wole putte to vs þat it is not profitable

62

ne worsshipful to vs for to leeuen oure lustes, and þat
alle wyse and worsshipful men of þis world trauaillen
for to geten hem eeses, and lustes, and worsshipe, and
greet loos in this world. And ȝef þat we deden   235
ooþerwyse men wolde blaamen vs, and scornen vs,
and sette riȝt nouȝt by vs. Ande þerfore it is
wysdom and worsship a man to confourme hym to
þe world, and also þat he mowe bee syker of his
lyfloode after his astaat þe whiles þat he lyueth.   240
þise ben þe skiles of þe world. But aȝens alle þise
enemys we haan good and trewe resouns ynowe which
þat Crist and hise lawes haan ytauȝt, wiþ þe which
we mown wel keepen vs fro þise ȝree forseide
cruele enemys and werreyours.   245
    And as anemptys þe feende Seynt Petir waarneþ
vs and teecheþ vs on þis wyse: he seith, "Breþeren, beþ
soobre and waaketh for ȝoure aduersaire þe deuel,
rooryng as a lyon, goth aboute seechyng whom he
may swolewen and distroyen, to whom withstoonde   250
ȝe stroonge in feith." So þat by þilke apostels counseil
we schuln withstoonden hym with byleeue. [f117r] And þat is a
trewe counseil, ffor oure byleeue teecheþ vs þat þe deuel
is a lyere and is alwey abouten to bigylen vs with his
falseheed, ffor we weeren ymaad for to serue God, and   255
ȝef þat we so doo and hoolden hise hestes and dyen
soo we shulne bee parteners of his blisse. And ȝef we
been recchelees of hym and breken hise hestes and dyen
so we shuln go to þe peyne of helle. And þouȝ þat
þe deuel byhote vs neuere so loonge lyf we schuln lyue   260
neuere þe lenger, and also þouȝ we myȝte lyue manye
þousand ȝeeres ȝet at þe laste we moten nedys dyen
and been ydeemed after oure werkes þat we haan ydoon
in oure lyf. And þerfore ȝef þat we haan wel ylyued
it is good þat we hoolden vs so til þat we dyen,   265
and ȝef þat we haan yuel ylyued it is tyme þat we
amende vs toward oure eende. And also þouȝ þat
God is mercyable and good þat shulde not with skyle
maaken vs þe booldere to synnen but it schulde
maaken vs þe moore besy to keepen vs fro synne,   270

63

ffor euere þe betere þat þe lord is þe betere he ouȝte
to been yserued. And in certein þere is noo lord þat
he ne wolde been yuel apayed ȝef þat his seruaunt
greuede hym þe wers for trust of þe lordis curteisye
275 and his meeknesse, ffor þat myȝte maaken a lord
ful sterne aȝens his seruaunt. And, þerfore, we mown
wel feele þat þe feendis teechyng is fals and wykkede
aȝens oure trewe bileeue. And þerfore with oure trewe
byleeue we shulden stedefastly withstoonden hym and
280 hise leesynges. ffor Seynt Iame seith, "Withstoonde
ȝe þe deuel and he shal flee from ȝowe." and þus
with þe grace of God we schuln maake þe strenge
enemye to flee. But we moten bee wel waar, for
þouȝ he flee at oo tyme he wole come aȝen with
285 anoother wyle, for he is ful of wyles. And also ȝef
þat oure flessh or þe world assaillen vs, þe feend
wol alwey bee with hem for to looke how þat he may
helpe to bigylen vs. And ȝef he may not doo to vs on
þis wyse he wole assaylen vs by oothere weyes by
290 hymself, or by meenes, as þus: he wol often assaye
to brynge a man in to glotonye, and ȝef he may not
brynge hym þerto he wole assaye to brynge hym to ouer
greet abstinence; or summe men he wole tempten to been
coueitous and besy abouten worldely þinges, and ȝef
295 he may not ouer comen hem þerinne he wole foonde to
bryngen hem in to þe synne of slouth; and summe he
foondeth to brynge in to wanhope, and ȝef he may not
doo that he assayeth to maake men synne þe moore for
trust of Goddis mercy. And þus þe feend from synne to
300 synne with manye temptaciouns besieth hym euere moore
for to drawen vs toward the broode wey of helle. And,
þerfore, we moten alwey bee [f117v] reedy for to withstoonden
hym with stroong feith. ffor of þise forseyde temptaciouns
oure byleeue teecheþ vs þat neythere glotonye, ne ouer
305 muchel abstinence been vertues, but þe meene bytwene
þise two is a vertue, and þat is mesurable taakyng of
mete and drynke for neede of oure kynde. And also
coueytyng to haaue to muchel of þe world is a vice,
and slouþe is a vice, and the meene bitwene þise two

64

is a greete vertue, and þat is for to trauaille trewely   310
for þat þat men needeth; and ȝef men geten moore
ouer þat for to helpe þerwith her needy breeþeren and
neiȝebours. And eeke it is a greete synne for to mystruste
in þe mercy of God, and it is a greet synne for
to synne þe moore for truste of Goddis mercy, and   315
ȝet þe meene of þise two is a greet vertue, and þat
is for to leeuen euel for dreede of God and for to
doo good for þe loue of God. And, þerfore, þus oure
bileeue shal teechen vs þe meene wey þat is vertue
bitwene þe extremites þat ben vices, to þe whiche þe   320
feend wole drawen vs from vertues and leeden vs in
to vices. And, þerfore, þus we moten walke in vertues
and withstoonde the feend stroongly with oure feith in
þise forseide temptaciouns, and in alle oothere. And
þanne shulne we þoruȝ swyche doynges haaue þank of   325
God and victorie of oure oolde enemy þe feend.
    And also we moten stryue stroongly aȝens oure
flesshe. ffor ȝef we folewen þe lykerousnesse of þe flesshe
or obeyen to his freelte he wol leeden vs in by þe wyde
ȝaate in to þe broode wey of helle. ffor as Seynt   330
Poul seith, "þe flessh coueiteth aȝens spirit and þe
spirit aȝens þe flessh, þise two coueiten eithere aȝens
oothere. And þe werkes of the flessh been vices and þe
fruyt of þe spirit is vertue." And, þerfore, he teecheþ vs
þat we shulde not walke after þe flessh but after þe   335
spirit. ffor he seith þat þe wysdom of þe flessh is
deeþ and þat þe wisdom of þe spirit is lyf and pees.
And þe wisdom of þe flessh is enemy to God, ne he
nys, ne he ne may not bee suget to the lawe of God.
And, þerfor, he seith to vs, "Ȝef we lyuen after þe   340
flessh we shulne dyen, þat is to seye, we shuln bee
dampned; and ȝef þat þoruȝ þe spirit we maken
deede þe deedys of oure flessh we shuln lyue," þat is
to seye, [f118r] we schuln bee saaued. And, þerfore, doo we
after þis trewe counseil of þe gospel and maake we   345
deede þe vices of þe flessh. ffor þe apostel teecheþ
vs, and also God of his goodnesse wole not þat we
maake deede oure flessh but þe deedis of oure flessh,

þe whiche been vices fiȝtyng aȝens the spirit. ffor
350 God of his greete curteisye wole þat we leete oure
flessh haaue al þat hym needeth skilfulliche and þat he
ordeyneþ for vs ynouȝ booþe mete and drynke and
clooþing. And he wole þat we taaken þerof in swyche
mesure as best is for vs. And whan we taaken
355 so þerof þat it dooþ vs harme, he hooldeþ hym
not apayed, but as a good leeche þat kepte not þat
þe seeke man tooke moore þanne shulde turne hym to
goode, al þouȝ þe seeke man desire ofte tymes to
taake and vse out of mesure aȝens his lyf and his
360 heele also. And, þerfore, ȝef we shuln in at þe strayte
ȝaate we musten keepe oure flessh in right reule as
men keepen a seek man þat is disposed to fallen into
woodnesse, hoopynge to bryngen hym to heele. ffor
oure flessh hath alwey þat seeknesse þat he is disposed
365 to be woode ȝef þat he haaue al þat he desireth.
And ȝef þat he weere woode þanne wolde he raþest
doon harme to hise nexte and hise beste freendis, for
þat is þe kynde of woodnesse. And, þerfore, with
good reule of þe spirit maake we deede þe vicious
370 lustes and werkes of þe flessh. And ȝeue we þe flessh
al þat is good for hym and no moore and þanne
shal he lyuen and been al hool. And so shuln we
euermoore lyuen togidere in eendeless blisse. And
þus shal þe goode hoope of vs maken vs to reule wel
375 oure flessh and keepen hym heere a lytel while from
his vnskilful lykerousnesse þe whiles þat we been heere
in þis soory world, in good hoope þat þe leest þing
þat we suffren now heere wilfully in oure flessh shalle
turne vs into muche moore blisse þanne al þat we kouden
380 deuyse heere vpon eerthe. And þus shuln we þoruȝ þe
grace of God and þoruȝ good hoope hoolde the flessh
vnder and walke after þe spirit in at þe streyte ȝaate
into þe narugh wey þat leedeþ to heuene.
    We moten also stryuen ful harde aȝens þe
385 worlde, þe whiche with folye and vanitee is ful besy
aboute to bryngen vs into þe broode wey þat leedeþ
to helle. And, þerfore, do we as Seynt Poul teecheþ,

66

ffor he biddeth vs þat we shulden sauoure þoo thynges
þat been aboue and not þoo thynges þat been heere on
eerth. [f118v] And, sikerly, ȝef we taaken good keepe þis is 390
a trewe counseil. ffor ȝef þat we byhoolden þe
thynges þat been aboue we shuln fynde þere oure
lord God and his blissed moodir, hise aungelis and
hise seyntes, with alle reeste, ioye, and pees withouten
any eende. And ȝef þat we bihoolden to þe thynges 395
þat been heere on eerth we shuln fynde þat þere is
no thyng withouten trauail, or dreede, or anger, or
sum diseese. And þerto al þat euere is geten heere
it passeth soone. And, therfore, for þe loue of God
sette we not oure hertes so muche vpon þe foule, 400
stynkyng muk of þis false, faillynge world. But with good
resoun we shulden haue greet sauour in þoo thynges þat
been abouen and louen hem with alle oure hertes, ffor
þei been goode, delitable, sikere, and lastyng. And,
certes, we shulden dispise and haate þise veyne thynges 405
of þe world, for þei been euele, vneesie, vnsikere, and
not lastynge. And eek þei ben contrarious to þe
thynges abouen. Also Seynt Iohn seiþ, "Loue ȝe
not þe world ne þoo thynges þat been in þe world,
ffor he þat loueth þe world þe charitee of God is not 410
in hym. ffor alle þing þat is in þe world it is lust
of flessh, or lust of eyen, or pruyde of lyf, þe
whiche is not of þe faadir of heuene but it is of
þe worlde." And Seynt Iame seith þat þe frensshipe
of this world is enemy to God. And he seith þat 415
who þat euer wole be maad frende of this world he
is ordeyned enemy to God. How myȝte we þanne doo
moore folie þanne for to loue þis wrecched world,
sithen we seen wel by teechyng of þise seyntes þat
þe loue of þe world shulde brynge vs fro þe 420
loue of oure fadir of heuene and maake vs hise
enemys? Preye we þanne hertely to oure lord God
þe fadir of heuene þat he ȝef vs grace for to louen

388 he] he he U.

67

hym and dispise þis world. ffor, sykerly, we mown
425 not wel loue hym as we shulden doo ʒef þat we
louen þe world, ffor þis world is ful of falsheede, vanitee,
and folie and al þis is contrarie to God. And also
þei þat setten here trust in þis world been alle disseyued.
And þei þat setten hooly here trust in God and in heuenely
430 þinges abouen, þei been euere siker and shuln lakke noo
þing þat is good for hem. And also þe world may ʒeue
noo þing to hise loueres þouʒ þei pleesen hym neuere
so muchel, ffor to hem þat he best loueth he may
ʒeue noo thyng but swiche as he cleepeth richesses and
435 worsshipes, þe whiche been myscleped soo. ffor ʒef it
weere trewely cleped men shulden clepe it sorewe
and shaame. ffor þat þat is cleped richesse it is greet
tra[f119r]uaill to geten it, and it is greet dreede to
keepen it, and to departe þerfro it is greet heuynesse,
440 so þat fro þe firste getynge to þe laste forgoyng it
is alle sorewe. And þei þat haan þe greete rychesses
of þis world þei been as ofte sithes ateened, as
ofte adrad, as ofte seeke, and as soone deede,
as þei þat haan noone swiche richesses. And whan
445 þei been deede it letteth hem to comen to heuene
moore þan it helpeth hem. ffor Crist seide þat it
was hard for a riche man to entre into þe kyngdom of
heuene. And, þerfore, þat muk of þis world þat is cleped
richesse it shulde bee cleped sorewe and noo richesse.
450 ffor whan þat we haan moost neede it may stoonde
vs in noo stede. And so by resoun we aughten for to
dispisen swiche richesses and bee besy abouten to
maken vs tresour in heuene as Crist biddeth, ffor
þat is sauoury tresor and shal neuer faile. And
455 þis tresour heere vpon eerthe is fals, and passyng, and
vnsauoury. And, þerfore, as Seynt Poul seiþ, and also
it is seid heere byfore, "Take we sauour in þoo þinges
þat been abouen in heuene." And with þe sauour of
hem we shuln dispise thise false, vnsauoury þinges þat
460 been heere vpon eerthe þe whiche wolden liʒtly, ʒef
þat we tooken sauour in hem, bryngen vs in to þe
broode wey of helle. ffor þider haþ þe sauour of

68

eerthely þinges ylad many oon. And þat witnesseth
Seynt Poul þere as he seith þus, "Thoo þat wolen bee
maad riche fallen in to temptacioun and in to þe   465
deuels panter and in to manye vnprofitable and
envious desirs þe whiche drawen men to manslauȝtre
and also bryngen men to los of body and of soule."
And, þerfore, by þis, and by manye oothere auctoritees,
and also by kyndely skile, we mown wel see þat þise   470
þat men clepen heere richesses been noone verrey
richesses but þing of nouȝt þat letteþ men to gederen
hem þe faire richesses of heuene, þe whiche been verrey
richesses. And, þerfore, taake we sauour in þe richesses
abouen and dispise we al þat is heere byneþe vpon   475
eerthe þat wolde letten vs to goo in þe streite wey
þat leedeþ to þe blisse of heuene. And also þe
worsshipes of þis wrecchide world þat men desiren so
greetly, ȝef þat we been wel avised, þei been noone
worsshipes, ne þei auȝten not with treuth to been   480
cleped worsshipes. And we mowne bee riȝt siker þat
bifore God, þat is verrey treuth, þei been neither
richesses ne worsshipes, ffor byfore God alle vertue is
worsshipe and alle synne is shame. And in þis world
it is euene þe reuers, ffor þe world holt hem worsshipful 485
þat been greete werrey [f119v] ours and fiȝteres and þat
distroyen and wynnen manye loondis, and waasten
and ȝeuen muche good to hem þat haan ynouȝ,
and þat dispenden oultrageously in mete, in drynke,
in clooþing, in buyldyng, and in lyuyng in eese, slouþe,   490
and many ooþere synnes. And also þe world worsshipeþ
hem muchel þat woln bee venged proudly and dispitously
of euery wrong þat is seid or doon to hem. And of
swyche folke men maken bookes and soonges and
reeden and syngen of hem for to hoolde þe mynde   495
of here deedes þe lengere heere vpon eerth, ffor þat
is a þing þat worldely men desiren greetly þat here
naame myghte laste loonge after hem heere vpon

494 swyche] swy U.

69

eerth. But what so euere þe world deemeþ of swiche
500 forseide folke leerne we wel þat God is souuerayn
treuþe and a trewe iuge þat deemeth hem riȝt shameful
byfore God and alle þe compaignie of heuene, ffor þere is
alle synne shame and vnworsshipe. And also swiche
folke þat wolden fayne lyuen meekeliche in þis world
505 and ben out offe swich forseid riot, noise, and stryf,
and lyuen symplely, and vsen to eten and drynken
in mesure, and to clooþen hem meekely, and suffren
paciently wroonges þat ooþere folke doon and seyn
to hem, and hoolden hem apayed with lytel good of
510 þis world, and desiren noo greet naame of þis
world, ne no pris ther of, swiche folke þe world
scoorneth and hooldeþ hem lolleris and loselis, foolis
and schameful wrecches. But, sikerly, God holdeth
hem moost wise and most worsshipful, and he wóle
515 worsshipen hem in heuene for euere whan þat þoo
þat þe world worsshipeþ shuln bee shaamed and pyned
for euere in helle, but ȝef þat þei amenden hem
heere eer þanne þei passen out of þis world. And,
þerfore, taake we sauour in þoo þinges þat been so
520 goode and so worsshipful abouen and recche we neuer
þouȝ þe world scoorne vs or hoolde vs wrecches,
ffor þe world scoorned Crist and heeld hym a fool.
And alle þat he suffrede paciently. And Seynt Poul
seith þat Crist suffrede for vs leeuynge vs ensaumple
525 þat we schulden so doo folewynge hise traaces. And,
therfore, folewe we hise traaces and suffre we paciently
þe scoornes of þe world as he dede, and þanne
wole he ȝeuen vs grace to comen in by þe narugh wey
to the worsshipfulle blisse that he regneth inne.
530   [f120r] And ȝef þat we folewen þe worsshipes of þis world,
as God forbeede, thei woln ful liȝtly bryngen vs by
þe broode wey in to þe schameful place þat þe feend
is inne, þat is, in to þe peyne of helle. Also it needeþ
vs greetly to bee ful wel waar þat we folewen not
535 euel companye of þis world, ne þat we confoorme vs
not þerto, ffor þat is a thinge þat myȝt liȝtly brynge
vs in to þe broode wey of helle. ffor ofte sithes euel

70

companyes bryngen men to synne whan þat þe feend,
þe flessh, ne the world shulden not bryngen hem þerto,
ȝef þat swiche euel companies ne weere. And þus ofte   540
tymes men goon to þe tauerne and been drunken or to
þe bordel and doon leccherye. And þere þei fiȝten
oþerwhile and doon manye oothere synnes for plesaunce
of yuel felasshipe þat þei folewen. And ȝet ne weere
swiche euel companye þat þei been inne in þat tyme   545
þei wolden not doo so neiþer for temptacioun of þe
feend, ne for likerousnesse of þe flessh, ne for vanyte
of þe world. And, þerfore, it seemeth þat in swiche
caas euele companie is worse þan any of þise
ȝre forseide enemys. And þat wot þe deuel ful wel.   550
And, þerfore, he dooþ as a foulere þat taaketh first a brid
and maakeþ þerof a wacchebrid and setteþ it bisyde his
net for to synge. And þanne whanne þat oother briddes
seen it and heeren it synge þei fallen alle doun to it.
And þe foulere draweþ his net and so taaketh hem.   555
And summe of hem he sleeþ, and summe he keepeþ to maake
wachbriddes of for to bigyle with alle the wachbriddes and
eeke þilke þat he taketh. And riȝt so þe feend, whan he
may taaken a leccherous man, he feedeth hym ofte with
þe foule lustes of his flessh and of þe worlde als. And   560
þanne he taakeþ hym and maakeþ of hym his wach for
þat he shulde with enticynge and euel ensaumple maaken
moo to fallen and to been ykauȝt in þe feendes net.
And so moo and moo til þat at þe laste he bryngeþ
hem alle þat he taakeþ to þe deeþ of soule, but ȝef   565
it so bee þat þei þoruȝ þe grace of God breken out
of his net and fleen vp to heuene ward. And, þerfore, it
is ful needful þat we preye besily to God þat he keepe
vs from euel companye lest þat we fallen adoun with hem
and been ykauȝt of oure oolde enemy, as he kauȝte Adam   570
oure forme fadir by entycynge of Eue his wif. And þoruȝ
þat ouercomynge of Adam þe feend gaat power of
alle mankynde til þe tyme þat oure blessede lord
Ihesu Crist suffrede harde deeþ for to [f120v] aȝenbuggen
mankynd out of his power. But now swiche as been   575
synful men and wacches of þe feend been cleped of þe

71

world "goode felawes". ffor þei þat woln waaste þe
goodis þat God hath sent hem, in pruyde of the world,
and in lustes of here flessh, and goon to þe tauerne
580 and to þe bordel, and pleyen at þe dees, waaken
loonge anyȝtes, and sweren faste, and drynken, and
ianglen to muche, scoornen, bakbiten, iaapen, gloosen,
boosten, lyen, fiȝten, and been baudes for here felawes,
and lyuen al in synne, and in vanitee, þei been hoolde
585 "goode felawes". And moore harme is þere is now in this
world muche swich curside felashipe. And, forsothe,
alle swiche felashipe walkeþ in þe broode wey þat
leedeþ to losse of body and of soule. And, as þe
gospel seith, ffewe men fynden þe nargh wey þat
590 leedeþ to blisse. And ȝet of þoo fewe, whan þei comen
amonges hem þat goon þe nargh wey and speken
to hem þat leeuen þe broode wey þat þei been inne
and conseillen hem to turne in to þe nargh wey
þat leedeþ to blisse, þei of þe broode wey been
595 comunliche encoumbred of hem, and scoornen hem,
mysseyn hem, and blamen hem, and hoolden with
oother þat mayntenen her euele deedes. And þei
been veery with þe felasshipe of hem þat hoolden
þe nargh wey. And ȝet, for al þat, þe nargh wey
600 is þe wey of God and þe broode wey is þe wey of þe
feende. And, neuerthelees, þe world clepeth hem
fooles þat goon Goddis weyes, and men clepen hem
"goode felawes" and worsshipful þat goon in þe feendis
weyes. And so in this world þe seruice of þe feend
605 is worsshiped and preised. And, þerfore, it is ful sooþ
þat Seynt Iohn seith þat alle þis world is set in euel.
And siþþe þat it so is, do we after Seynt Poul
þat biddeþ vs þat we shulden not bee in wille to
bee maad lich to þis world. And, þerfore, dispise
610 we þis wrecchide, fals world þat is alle set in euel
and taake we sauour in þoo þinges þat been abouen,
þe whiche been alle goode. And on þis wise, as it is
seid byfore, withstoonde we þe feend with stroong feiþ,
and hoolde we þe flessh vndir with good hoope, and
615 dispise we þe world with þe charitee of God and þe

72

blisse of heuene, and þanne shuln we, with Goddis grace,
goon in at þe streite ȝaate and so goo forth in þe
nargh wey þe whiche shal with Goddis mercy bringen
vs to þe blisse of heuene. And whan þat God of
his greete goodnesse haþ ȝeuen vs grace to comen   620
in to þe nargh wey þanne it is good þat we
hoolden vs þer inne and þat we fallen not out of
it in to þe broode wey, þat is þat we keepe þe
comaundementȝ of God and þat we breeke hem for noo
þing. For [f121r] as it is seyde heere bifore, the nargh wey is 625
þe keepyng of Goddis comaundementȝ, and þe broode wey
is þe brekynge of þe selue comaundementȝ. And, þerfore,
we shuln vndirstoonde þat þer been ten comaundementȝ,
the whiche been þise þat folewen next after. The
firste is þat we shuln haue noon oother God but oure   630
lorde God of heuene. þe seconde is þat we shuln not
taake þe naame of oure lorde God in veyn. The þridde
is þat we shuln halewe oure haliday. The feerþe is
þat we shuln worsshipen our fadir and oure moodir.
The fifthe is þat we shuln slee no man. The sixte is   635
þat we shuln doo noo leccherye. The seuenthe is þat
we shuln not steele. The eighthe is þat we shuln bere
noo fals witnesse aȝens oure neiȝebour. The nyenthe
is þat we shulne not coueyte oure neiȝebores hous.
The tenthe is þat we shuln not desire oure neiȝebores   640
wyf, ne his seruant, ne his mayden, ne his oxe, ne
his asse, ne noo þing of his. And of thise ten
comaundementȝ þe ȝree firsre been appered to þe
loue and þe worsshipe of God, and þe oothere
seuene folewyng to oure euene cristene. And, þerfore,   645
taake we alwey riȝt greete keepe of þise forseyde
hestes and þat we breken noone of hem. ffor alle
þei þat been in any fals byleeue or doon ydolatrie or
wichecrafte, or louen, or dreden, or worsshipen any
thyng moore þan God, þei breken þe firste comaundement.   650
And alle þei þat taaken þe name of God falsly or in

620 ȝeuen] ȝouen U.

73

veyn, þei breken þe secounde comaundement. And alle
þei þat setten hem not on þe hooliday to þe seruice
of God and keepen hem not fro werchyng of eerthly
655 werkes at here power, or þat dispenden þe halyday
in worldly besynesse, in flesshly lustes, or in merth
of vanitee, þei breken þe ʒridde comaundement, And
all þoo þat worsshipen not here fadir or here moodir,
or þat helpen hem or counforten hem not in body and in
660 soule in here neede at here power, or þei þat worsshipen
not here gostly moodir holy chirche as þei auʒten to
doo, þei breken þe feerth comaundement. Ande alle
þoo þat sleen any man in þouʒt, in woord, or in deede,
þei breken þe fifthe comaundement, but ʒef it been
665 swiche as haan auctorite by good resoun for to putte
men þerto that disseruen þe deeth by Goddis lawe,
and ellis not. And alle þoo þat donn lecchery in any
degre, kyndely or vnkyndly, þei breken þe sixte commaundement.
And alle þoo þat robben or stelen, taa[f121v]ken by maistrie,
670 or be extorcoun, or by any gyle, or falsheede here neiʒebores
goodis, þei breken þe seuenþe comaundement. And alle
þoo þat beren falsse witnesse aʒens here neiʒebore, or
sclaundren, or bacbyten hem falsly in euel, þei breken
þe eightþe comaundement. And alle þoo þat coueiten
675 here neiʒebores hous, land, or any thyng of his oonly for þe
coueityng of it, þei breken þe nyenþe comaundement.
And alle þoo þat desiren here neiʒebores wyf or
housebonde, seruant or mayden, alle be it so þat
þei geten not þat þei desiren, ʒet for þe desirynge
680 þei breken þe tenþe comaundement. And also alle þei
þat breken any of þise forseide comaundementʒ þei been
in þe broode wey þat leedeth to helle, til þat þei
repenten hem þerof and been in ful wille to kepe
alle þe forseide comaundementʒ at here power in to
685 here lyues eende. And so it is ful parillous to
breken hem and ful profitable to keepen hem. But
worldly and flesshly men þenken þat þe comaundementʒ
been ful harde to keepe. But, sikerly, þei þat been
goostly and louen wel God þinken hem not heuy to
690 keepe. ffor Seint Iohn seith þat it is þe charge of

74

God þat we keepe hise comaundementȝ, and hise
commaundementȝ been not heuy. And, þerfore, ȝef
we louen God, as we auȝten to doo, we shuln alwey
keepen þoo ten comaundementȝ with louyng and
dreedyng hym as oure fadir and oure lorde, and oure   695
neiȝebore as oure self. And þat we mown wel knowe
by þe woordis of Crist þat seide to a man þat
askide hym what was þe gretteste comaundement in
þe lawe. And Ihesu answerde and seide, "Thou
shalt loue þi lord God of alle þin herte, of alle   700
þin soule, of alle þi mynde, and of alle þi strengthes; this is
þe firste and þe gretteste commaundement. The seconde
is lyke to þis: þou shalt loue þi neiȝebour as þi
self. And in þise two commaundementȝ hangeþ alle þe
lawe and þe prophetes." And sithen þat we mown with þe   705
louyng of God and of oure neighebour keepen alle þe
commaundementȝ of God, we auȝten not þanne hoolden it
heuy for to keepen hise hestes, ne we shulden not grucchen
to keepen hem on þat wise. ffor, sikerly, it is resonable,
delitable and profitable for to loue God abouen alle oothere   710
þinges and oure neiȝebour as oure self. Resounable it is for of
nouȝt he ma[f122r]ade vs to his owene ymage and lyknesse, and
he hath ordeyned vs ȝef þat we woln our self to be
parteneres with hym of þe blisse of heuene. And al þat is
here vpon eerthe he hath ordeyned it for þe helpe and þe   715
eese of vs. And al þat we haan þat good is he ȝeueth it
vs. And al þat we asken hym with a good, trewe herte
þat skilful is he graunteth it vs. And whanne þat we
hadden lost, þoruȝ þe synne of Adam, oure part of
paradis he coom þanne for loue of vs, and tooke flessh and   720
bloode of þe blesside mayden Marie, and bicoom man for
vs, and was born of þat blesside mayden withouten wem of
hire maydenhoode. And þe tyme of his blesside berthe was
in þe cooldeste of þe wynter, and in a poore logge
and a coolde. And whanne þat he was born his   725
blesside moodir wrappide hym in a fewe poore clooþis
and leyde hym in a maungeour bitwene an oxe and an
asse for to warmen hym, for þere was no grettere aray.
And he coom on so poore and so meeke a wise into

730 þis world al for to ȝeuen vs ensaumple of meeknesse
and of wilful pouerte. And þe eiȝteþe day after his
burthe he was circumcised and shedde for vs þoo
of his precious blood. And after þat he wonede heere
vpon eerthe moore þanne two and ȝritty wynter, and
735 prechede and tauȝte þe poeple þe riȝte wey to heuene,
and wrouȝte monye wondres, and heelede muchel
folke booþe bodyly and goostly, and suffrede heete
and coolde, and þirst booþe weet and drie, and euel
heberewe scoornes, repreues, bacbitynges, chidynges,
740 wroonges, and manye oothere dispites and greete
diseeses. And at þe laste his owene disciple bytrayed
hym for his goodnesse. And afterwarde þei tooken hym,
and bounden hym as a þeef, and ladden hym to here
bisshop, and þere þei acusiden hym with fals witnesse,
745 and buffeteden hym, and blyndefelden hym, and
scoorneden hym, and spitteden on hys blisside face
as þei wolden haue donn on a dogge. And after þat
he was ylad bifore Pilat of Pounce, and þere he
was falsly accused and enprisouned, and afterward
750 ystript naaked, and bounden to a piler, and beeten
with scharpe scoorges, til þat al his blesside boody
ran on bloode þat neuere dede synne. And after [f122v]
þei setten on his blesside heed a coroune of greete
scharpe þornes, and clooþiden hym as a fool, and
755 scorneden hym. And after þat þei deemeden hym
falsly to þe deeth, and maaden hym go bitwene two
þeeues as weery and al forbled as he was, and maden
hym to bere hys heuy cros þat he shulde dyen on
vpon his owene bak þoruȝ þe citee in siȝte of his
760 blissede moodir, his kyn, and his oothere freendis.
And whanne þat he coom in to þe place of comun
iustyse þei naylleden his blessed feet and hise hoondis
with greete boistouse naylles to þe cros, and al to
drowen his hooly lymes vpon þe cros. And ȝet in alle

739 heberewe] herberewe U.
762 iustyse] iuyse U.

76

hise greete peynes þis innocent preyede for hise enemys   765
and seide, "ffadir, for ȝeue hem þis gilt for þei witen
not what þei doon." And þoo þei heengen oo þeef on
his riȝt half and anooþer on his lyft half, and hym
for dispit þei heengen bytwene hem two. And þanne he
þirstede soore for þe greete peynes þat he hadde   770
suffred and þe bleedynge þat he hadde bled, and þoo
þei ȝeeuen hym eysel and galle for to drynke. And
whanne he hadde assayed what it was he wolde not
drynke it but boowide his blessede heed adoon and
ȝelde vp þe goost. And þanne þere coom a knyȝt   775
ycleped Longeus and smoot hym þoruȝ þe herte with a
spere, and þer coom out waatir and bloode. And
alle þis he suffrede for vs. And after þis hise blesside
body was taaken doon of þe cros and buried. And
þanne he wente doun in to helle, and þere he fette   780
out þilke þat he louede. The thridde day after he
aroos froom deeth to lyue and schewede hym to manye
men and wommen, and þat on manye wyses. And after,
in þe siȝte of hise disciples, he steigh vp in to heuene.
And now of his greete goodnesse he keepeþ vs fro   785
manye parils and we greeuen hum ful soore euery day.
And ȝet he spaareth vs to loke whether we woln amende
vs with long tyme. And þouȝ we synnen neuere so greetly,
anoon as we been riȝt soory þerof, and in ful wyl to
synnen no moore, anoon he forȝeueth vs gladly. And,   790
þerfore, whan we biþenken vs wel vpon þise forseide
þinges þe whiche þat God of his greete goodnesse hath
doon and dooth euery day for vs, and vpon þe harde
peynes þat he hath suffred for vs, we mown [f123r] wel
knowen þat it is resounable to loue God obouen alle   795
oothere þinges, as it is seide bifore. And also it is

770 þat he hadde...] A. *begins*.
771 and þe] and for þe A.
780 fette] fecchede A.
782 froom] fro A.
790 forȝeueth] forȝiueþ hit A.

77

resounable þat we louen oure neiӡebour as oure self,
ffor it is þe wil and þe commaundement of God
þat we so doo. And eek oure neighbour is of þe selue
800 forme and kynde þat we been of, and þerfore
kyndly we shulden iche oon hertely loue oothere with
good skile. And also it is delitable for to loue God
abouen alle oother þinges and oure neiӡebour as oure
self. ffor who þat loueþ God ouer alle þing he may
805 wel deliten hym in þenkynge þat he loueth hym þat
passeth alle ooþere þinges, in goodnesse, in fairnesse,
in konnyng, and in myӡt, and þat God of his
greete goodnesse wole louen hym aӡen a þousand
fold better þan any herte kan þenken or deuysen.
810 And ӡet þerto he shal haaue þe loue of alle þe
companye of heuene and of alle þe good folke on
eerthe. And þat shal not passe as worldly loue dooþ,
but it shal laste euere with outen eende. And to
louen oure neiӡebour as oure self it is ful merye
815 booþ to body and to soule, so þat þe loue of God
and of oure neiӡebour it is ful of merthe and it
is of grettere delite þan is any oother þing. And
also it is profitable to loue God abouen alle
oothere þinges and oure neiӡebour as oure self, for
820 he þat dooþ so shalle haue þe blisse of heuene þat
euere shal laste. And þat is þe althergretteste
profit þat may bee. And, þerfore, siþþen þat þe
loue of God and of oure neiӡebour is so resounable,
delitable, and profitable, as it is preued here
825 bifore, we been to greete foolis but ӡef we keepen
vs with alle oure myӡt in þat loue, ffor þat is
þe nargh wey þat leedeth to heuene, of þe whiche

797 neiӡebour] neiӡebors A.
801 iche oon] euurichone A.
813 euere] A. *omits.*
825 ӡef] A. *omits.*
827 whiche] whuche hit A.

is spoken of heer to fore. And, þerfore, preye we
hertely to oure lord Ihesu Crist þat of his muchel
mercie he ʒeue vs grace to commen into þat wey and   830
to hoolden vs þerinne. But þere is muche folk þat
seyn þat þei ben in þat wey whan it is not so,
ffor þe speche of alle is þat þei louen God abouen
alle oothere þinges. But, what so euere þei seyn,
Crist, þat may not lyen, seiþ þus, "Who þat loueþ   835
me schal keepe my woordes and my commaundementʒ,
and my fadir shal louen hym, and we shullen commen
to hym and maake oure dwellynge with hym. And
who þat loueþ not me keepeþ not my woordis." Also
Crist seiþ þus, "He þat hath myne commaundementʒ   840
and keepeth hem, þat is he þat loueth me." [f123v] And
Seynt Iohn seiþ, "In þat we witen þat we knowen
God ʒef þat we keepen hise commandementʒ. And
who seith þat he knoweþ God and keepeþ not hise
comaundementʒ, he is a lyere and treuth is not   845
in hym." And also he seith, "Loue we not with woord
ne with toonge, but with deede and with treuth."
And, þerfore, we mown wel knowe by thise woordis
of Crist, and of his apostles, and by manye oothere
auctorites of hooly writte, þat noo man may come   850
to þe blisse of heuene but ʒef he be in wille to keepe
þe commaundementʒ of God, þe whiche comaundementʒ
been fully kept of hem þat louen God and here
neiʒebour as hem self, as þei auʒten to donn, and
as it is seid bifore. And, þerfore, alle þoo þat   855
louen so God and here neiʒebour as hem self þei been

828 heer to fore] herbi fore A.
845 comaundementʒ] hestes A.
846 also] A. *omits*.
851 he] U. *omits*.
852 comaundementʒ (2nd)] A. *omits*.
853 God] god ouur alle þing A.
854 þei] hem A.
856 neiʒebour] neihʒebores A. / as hem self] A. *omits*.

in þe nargh wey þat leedeþ to þe blisse þat euere
shalle lasten. And alle þoo þat loue not so God
and here neiȝebour þei been in þe broode wey þat
860 leedeþ to þe deeth of helle peyne þat euere shalle
lasten. And, þerfore, lifte we vp oure hertes to
oure lord God alle myȝty þat hath maad vs and
bouȝt vs with his precious blood. And preye we hym
hertely of his greete goodnesse and of his eendeles
865 mercy þat he ȝef vs grace to keepen vs out of
þat broode wey þat leedeþ to þe griseliche peynes
of helle, and graunt vs grace to goon in þat nargh
wey þat leedeth to þe blisse of heuene, til þat
we comen to þat blisse þat he hath ordeyned for
870 hem þat louen hym. Amen.

860 deeth of helle peyne] pyne of helle A.
868 þe] A. *omits* / þat (2nd)] A. *omits*.
869 þat blisse þat] þulke ioye whuch A.
870 Amen] A. *omits*.

COMMENTARY

I THE BOKE OF CUPIDE

title: The title "The Cuckoo and the Nightingale" is attested by Ff.T.Th., and was followed by editors up to and including Skeat, who fancied it was imitated from Hoccleve's *Letter of Cupid* (p.lviii). The titles in Ff. and T. are inserted in later hands and may have been imitated from Th. F. and B. are earlier, and generally better texts, so they are followed. S. has no title.

1-20   Descriptions emphasising the irresistible power of the god of love are commonplace in medieval litera-ture: compare, for example, *Le Roman de la Rose* 865-906, Froissart's *Le Cour de May* 699-761, and Machaut's *Le Dit du Vergier* 246-324. If these lines were derived directly it may have been from *Le Dit du Vergier*, for lines 3, 6-8, 9-10, 11-12, 13, 14, 16-17, 18-19 may all be parall-eled there; but all are commonplace.

1-2   *The Canterbury Tales* I, 1785-6. The phrase "For he can make..." (I, 1789) repeated at 3, 5, 8, 13 appears to have stuck in this author's mind.

26-7   Perhaps imitated from F. *Prologue to the Legend of Good Women* 37-8; but compare also *Canterbury Tales* VII 3201-2.

30-33   Some of the recognisable symptoms of lovesick-ness. Compare *The Canterbury Tales* I, 1356-79; and see J.L.Lowes *Modern Philology* XI, 1913, 491-546.

37   olde and vnlusty: It is difficult to know how serious such references are. Both Chaucer (*Lenvoy de Chaucer a Scogan* 29-36) and Gower (*Confessio Amantis* VIII 2403) represent themselves perhaps mockingly as too old for love; but both were fairly old when these poems were written. If I am right about the authorship and date of this poem, Sir John Clanvowe would have been in his late forties when he wrote it.

81

39   hote and colde, an accesse euery day: The medically
correct, standard terminology for referring to the
cotidian fever. Compare Trevisa's *Bartholomew* p.90: "þe
ffebre cotidiana...ffurst þe colde & þer after þe hete,
and euery day axesse; ӡit wers, for somday comeþ many
strong accesse". For *accesse* applied to lovesickness
see *MED* acces(se) n. 2a.

41   shaken: See Variants. This reading is preferable to
F.B.'s "slayn", because *shaken* is the word more usually
used in this context. Compare *Complaint of the Black
Knight* 136-7, *Troy Book* V 601.

   feueres white: "lovesickness". Cotgrave defines it
thus: "'Fievres blanches', the agues where with maidens
that have the green sickness are troubled; hence 'Il a
les fievres blanches' either he is in love, or sick with
wantoness" (quoted by Skeat, *Oxford Chaucer* II, 466).

47-50   Fairly clearly the author refers to a proverb
(see Whiting N 111). Compare "On the third of April come
in the cuckoo and the nightingale" and "The nightingale
and the cuckoo sing both in one month" (*Oxford Dictionary of Proverbs* pages 452, 651), but both seem to be
later. On the importance for lovers of the nightingale's
song see particularly *The Floure and the Leafe* 39-42.

55   the thirde nyght of May: May 3rd was one of the
"unlucky" days (see J.M.Manly ed. *The Canterbury Tales*,
1931, p.551) mentioned several times in Chaucer (*Canterbury Tales* I 1462-3, VII, 3187-90). It is the day on
which Pandarus suffers his "teene in love" (*Troilus and
Criseyde* II 56-63), and is here unlucky for the poet
since he hears the cuckoo sing before the nightingale.

67   crepe: See Variants; and compare a similar use of
this word in *Piers Plowman* B, XX, 43.

78-80   How the belief that birds chose their mates on
St Valentine's Day grew up is not certain, but the
belief was well established by this time in England, and
appears frequently in poetry: see *The Parliament of*

82

Fowls 386-9; *Compleynt d' Amours* 85-91; *Cinkante Ballades* Nos.XXXIV and XXXV.

80   Marche: Skeat read "feverere" following T.Th.; but the other texts read *Marche*, and it appears that St Valentines's day could fall in March though it more usually fell in February. *The Nuremberg Chronicle*, 1493, gives March 16th as his feast day (see Ruth Webb Lee, *A History of Valentines*, 1953, p.3).

82-3   Perhaps an echo of *The Parliament of Fowls* 202-3.

90   lewede cukkowe: An adjective applied to the cuckoo on two other occasions in this poem (50, 103), and also elsewhere. Compare *The Parliament of Fowls* 616 "Go, lewed be thow, whil the world may dure".

108-9   Considered by Vollmer (p.51) an echo of the *G. Prologue to the Legend of Good Women* 139-40; but this was disputed by J.L.Lowes (*PMLA* XX, 1905, 754 note 2).

113-5   The cuckoo's song was proverbially boring because it lacks variety (see Whiting C 600, 601). In Richard Nichol's poem *The Cuckoo* (1607), which perhaps makes use of *The Boke of Cupide* since it consists of a singing contest between a cuckoo and a nightingale, the cuckoo's song causes "laughter" among the assembled birds because of its monotony. *elynge* here probably means "tedious", "dull" (see *MED* elenge adj. 1b).

118-120   Here *pleyn* probably means "pertaining to plain-song, monophonic as opposed to polyphonic". This adjective is used of the cuckoo's song in *A Midsummer Night's Dream* III i 134: "The plain song cuckoo gray". *breke* probably means "trill" or "modulate" the notes of a song. Alexander Neckham,*De Laudibus Divinae Sapientiae* ed. T. Wright, RS 1863, p.391 says that the nightingale "breaks" the notes as it sings. At issue seem to be the rival merits of the monophonic and polyphonic styles of music which were frequently compared, for example, in *The Cloud of Unknowing* ed. Phyllis Hodgson, EETS OS, 218, 1944, p.101 and *The Owl and the Nightingale* 309-22.

124-135 *ocy, ocy*: A fairly frequently used imitation of the nightingale's song, though this seems to be its first use in English. This author may have taken it from Froissart (*Poésies* ed. A.Scheler, Brussels 1871, II 424) or from Deschamps (*Oeuvres* II 203, III 342). *ocy* was usually taken to be the imperative of *occire* "to kill". Compare *Receuil de Motets Francais* ed. G.Raynaud, Paris 1881, p.49:

> "Et si orrons le roussignol chanter
>   En l'ausnoi,
>   Qui dit; Oci ceus qui n'ont le cuer gai,
>   Douce Marot, grief sont li mau d'amer."

See further Otto Glauning ed. *Lydgate's Minor Poems*, EETS ES 80 1900, pp.36-8.

166-7 Compare *The Owl and the Nightingale* 839-44, for a similar debating stratagem.

178-80 See Variants. The F.B. reading fails to give a true rhyme or adequate sense. Skeat renders the passage as follows "The sense is 'For he who gets a little bliss of love may very soon find that his heir has come of age, unless he is always devoted to it'. This is a mild joke, signifying that he will soon find himself insecure, like one whose inheritance is threatened" (p.528).

184-5 "You will be as others who are forsaken, and then you will be called what I am called, that is, a cuckold". For the pun on "cuckoo" and "cuckold" see *La Messe des Oiseaus* 310-12, and *The Canterbury Tales* IX 243-56. See also Whiting C 603.

201-2 Proverbial, Whiting C 634.

204 A commonplace accusation; compare *Le Roman de la Rose* 1034-51, *F. Prologue to Legend of Good Women* 352-6.

209 *not oon worde more*: This is tantamount to an admission of defeat on the nightingale's part, for it was the rule of medieval school's debate that whoever argued his adversary into silence was the victor. Compare *The*

Owl and the Nightingale 391-410, 665-6; and *Dispute between a Good Man and the Devil* 949-52.

216-20   The offending cuckoo is twice driven off in *La Messe des Oiseaux* 146-9, 311-7. But perhaps the narrator is not wholly triumphant, for it appears to have been proverbially unlucky to throw things at the cuckoo. Whiting C 603 quotes Henry Medwall's *Fulgens and Lucres* (c.1497):

> "By cokkis bonis for it was a kocko,
> And men say amonge
> He that throwyth stone or stycke
> At suche a byrde he is lycke
> To synge that byrdes songe."

222   *papyngay*: The implication of the cuckoo's jibe is not clear. It may be he is implying the narrator is wanton, for the parrot has this reputation: compare Vincent of Beauvais, *Speculum Naturale* chapters XV and CXXXV: and *The Parliament of Fowls* 359 "The popiniay, ful of delicasye". But the word here may be used as a term of contempt, "as typical of vanity and empty conceit, in allusion to the bird's gaudy plumage or its mechanical repitition of words and phrases", though according to *OED popinjay* 4b, this is a later meaning (first use 1528).

237   *leve*: See Variants. The unique S. reading is adopted because it provides better sense in the context.

243   *daysye*: Probably an allusion to the daisy as a symbol of true womanhood. There was evidently a courtly cult devoted to this flower, both in France and England (see J.L.Lowes, *PMLA*, XIX, 1904, 593-683). This author perhaps took his ideas from the F. *Prologue to the Legend of Good Women* 40-210.

247   *thy songes*: See Variants. If *thy* is correct it would appear that the song referred to is perhaps by the author of *The Boke of Cupide*. However, no song beginning "I shewe hem al that be to love vntrue" appears to survive.

85

270 For a long account of the cuckoo's evil nature see
La Messe des Oiseaus 381-416, and *The Parliament of
Fowls* 358, 612-16. The cuckoo is unnatural (*vnkynde*) because it does not look after its own young but lays its
eggs in another bird's nest. The newly hatched cuckoo
then ejects its foster parents' young.

283 *maple that is feire and grene*: The maple was
"grown for shade and ornament" (*OED maple* 1), and it
seems to be these properties the poet has in mind here.
If the tree is meant to have a symbolic importance, it
may be the poet has in mind Pliny's notion (*Historia
Naturalis* XXIV xxxi) that maple-root in wine was good
for alleviating sadness.

284-5 *the Quene/At Wodestok*: If my notions about the
date of the poem are right a reference to Anne of Bohemia who was at Woodstock with Richard II in 1389 and almost certainly at other times as well (see E.Marshall,
The Early History of Woodstock Manor, 1873, pp.104, 441).

287 *hawthorn*: The hawthorn is usually associated with
constancy in love, as in *The Temple of Glas* 510-22; and
the nightingale, fittingly, sits in the hawthorn to sing
in *The Court of Love* 1353-4.

290 Compare *Troilus and Criseyde* II 64-70 where Pandarus is woken by the singing of the birds. But this ending
was probably suggested by *The Parliament of Fowls* 693-5.

II THE TWO WAYS

title: I have supplied the present title. The compiler
of the table of contents on ff.4r-4v refers to the treatise as "*de viis duabus*" but Clanvowe is unlikely to have
used a Latin title.

2-3 *the greete see*: Here probably the Mediterranean,
though also sometimes applied to the Black Sea. The
implied contrast is with the much smaller Sea of Marmora.

5-12   For the question see Luke xiii 23-4 which also has an abbreviated form of the answer. For the full answer see Matthew vii 13-44.

25-8   I Corinthians ii 9.

53-6   Psalm xxv 9, 4.

62-4   For the proverbial attachment of a fool to his bauble see Whiting F 394.

77-80   I Corinthians iii 19.

84-7   Psalm xvii 5.

90-2   Psalm cxxviii 1.

97-100   Matthew xix 16-17 but abbreviated.

107-9   Psalm cxi 10; but compare also Proverbs i 7, ix 10.

120-1   Perhaps Psalm cxix 21.

208-9   Psalm lxxxv 9.

246-51   I Peter v 8-9.

253-4   þe deuel is a lyere: John viii 44; but proverbial, see Whiting D 186.

280-1   James iv 7.

305-21   þe meene: Many proverbs celebrating the virtue of "the mean" are extant; see in particular Whiting M 443 "Mean is a virtue", and V 45 and W 117.

330-6   Galations v 16-25 but abbreviated.

336-9   Romans viii 6-7.

340-3   Romans viii 13.

349-53   Ecclesiasticus xxix 21, expanded at xxxix 26. But a common idea; see, for example, *Piers Plowman* B I 20-25.

387-90   Colossians iii 2.

408-14   I John ii 15-16.

414-7   James iv 4.

446-8   Probably Matthew xix 23; but compare Mark x 23-4, Luke xviii 24.

451-6   Perhaps loosely based on Matthew vi 19-20.

463-8   I Timothy vi 9.

523-5   I Peter ii 21.

565-7   Perhaps suggested by Psalm cxxiv 7. Compare also Psalm xci 3 and Proverbs vi 5.

577-85   *goode felawes*: Compare Chaucer's ironic use of this phrase (*Canterbury Tales* I 395, 650, 653; III 618, 1385) where it bears not only its literal meaning but connotes rascality as well.

605-6   Perhaps I John v 19.

607-9   Romans xii 2.

626-42   Exodus xx 3-17, but almost certainly known otherwise.

690-2   I John v 3.

694-705   Matthew xxii 36-40, but augmented from Luke x 27 or Mark xii 30 for "alle þi strengthes". Christ is quoting Deuteronomy vi 5.

742-79   Based on John xix, the only account in which Christ asks for a drink (28), bows his head (30), and is pierced so that blood and water come from his side (34). But Christ's words at 766-7 are from Luke xxiii 34.

776   *Longeus*: St Longinus, the name given to the soldier who pierced Christ's side. Traditionally cured of blindness and converted to Christianity by a drop of the precious blood, he became a monk in Caesarea in Cappadocia, converted many pagans, and finally was tried for his faith and beheaded.

834-9   John xiv 23-4.

88

'839–41   John xiv 21.

841–6   I John ii 3-4.

846–7   I John iii 18.

SELECT BIBLIOGRAPHY

i Editions

The Boke of Cupide appears under the title of "The Cuckoo and the Nightingale" in Thynne's 1532 edition of Chaucer's works, and in all subsequent editions up to the Bell edition of 1854. These have been listed and described by Eleanor P.Hammond, *Chaucer— A Bibliographical Manual*, 1908, pp.116-49. There have been four later editions of the poem:

ELLIS, F.S. *The Floure and the Leafe and the Cuckow and the Nightingale*, 1896.
SKEAT, W.W. *Chaucerian and Other Pieces*, 1897, pp.347-58 (Vol.VII of the *Oxford Chaucer*).
VOLLMER, E. *Das Mittelenglische Gedicht "The Boke of Cupide"* (Berliner Beitrage zur Germanischen und Romanischen Philologie XVII, Germanische Abteilung No.8, 1898).
SCATTERGOOD, V.J. *"The Boke of Cupide*— An Edition", *English Philological Studies*, IX, 1965, 47-83.

The Two Ways has been printed once:

SCATTERGOOD, V.J. *"The Two Ways*— An Unpublished Religious Treatise by Sir John Clanvowe", *English Philological Studies*, X, 1967, 33-56.

Information on the B.M. MS Additional 22283 fragment and variant readings were supplied by E.Wilson, *English Philological Studies*, XI, 1968, 54-6.

ii Books and Articles

SKEAT, W.W. "The Canon of Chaucer's Works" *Academy*, 1894, 67.
SKEAT, W.W. "The Author of the Cuckoo and the Nightingale", *Academy*, 1896, 365.

KITTREDGE, G.L. "Chaucer and Some of his Friends", *Modern Philology*, I, 1903, 1-18.

WAUGH, W.T. "The Lollard Knights", *Scottish Historical Review*, XI, 1914, 55-92.

BRUSENDORFF, A. *The Chaucer Tradition*, 1924, pp.441-4.

WARD, L.C. "The Authorship of the Cuckoo and the Nightingale", *MLN*, XLIV, 1929, 217-26.

ROBBINS, R.H. "The Findern Anthology", *PMLA*, LXIX, 1954, 610-42.

SEATON, M.Ethel. *Sir Richard Roos— Lancastrian Poet*, 1961, pp.388-92.

BREWER, D.S. *Chaucer in his Time*, 1963, pp.226-30.

SCATTERGOOD, V.J. "The Authorship of *The Boke of Cupide*", *Anglia*, LXXXII, 1964, 37-49.

LAMPE, D.E. "Tradition and Meaning in *The Cuckoo and the Nightingale*", in *The Art and Age of Geoffrey Chaucer* ed. J.Gardner and N.Joost, 1967, pp.49-62.

COTTLE, A.B. *The Triumph of English*, 1969, pp.248-57.

McFARLANE, K.B. *Lancastrian Kings and Lollard Knights*, 1972, pp.139-232.

GLOSSARY

THIS SELECTIVE GLOSSARY explains only words and senses now unfamiliar. In the arrangement ȝ follows *g*, but þ is treated as *th*; consonantal and vocalic *i* are treated together; *u* and *v* are not separated according to function. Where more than one form of the head-word is given the meaning relates to the first form.

accesse   n. attack of fever.
adrad   pp. afraid.
affrayed   pp. alarmed.
agryse   inf. quake with terror.
aȝenbuggen   inf. redeem.
althergretteste   sup. adj. greatest of all.
amayed   pp. terrified.
anemptys   prep. concerning.
apayed   pp. pleased, satisfied.
apeyre   inf. suffer harm.
appered   pp. appropriate to.
astaat   n. estate.
ateened   pp. grieved, annoyed.
awreke   pp. avenged.

babel(is)   n. bauble, jester's sceptre.
baudes   n. procurers.
benymen   inf. deprive.
biþenken   1. pl. pr. consider.
bordel   n. brothel.
bouȝt   pp. redeemed.
bowe   inf. bow, turn aside; bowen 3.pl. pr.; boowide
      3.s. pt.
brek   inf. trill.
byhote   3.s. pr. subj. promise.

cherles   n. churl's.
clepe   inf. be called; cle(e)peth, cleepeþ 3.s. pr.;
      clepen 3.pl. pr.; cle(e)ped pp.
coude   3.pl. pt. knew.
coueityng   n. desire.

coueyte   inf. desire eagerly, lust for; coueiteth 3.s.
           pr.; coueiten 3.pl. pr.

disese, dysese, diseesis   n. discomfort.
dispenden   3.pl. pr. spend.

eire   n. heir.
elynge   adj. tedious.
encoumbred   pp. hampered, entangled.
euene cristene   n. phr. fellow Christians.
eysel   n. vinegar.

fayne   adv. happily.
fayne   adj. happy; faynere comp. adj. happier.
fere   n. company.
fette   3.s. pt. fetched.
foonde   inf. try, attempt; foondeth 3.s. pr.
forbled   pp. having bled a lot.
forme   adj. first.

gederen   inf. gather.
gloosen   3.pl. pr. flatter, speak deceitfully.
goostly   adv. spiritually.
goostly   adj. spiritual.
grede   1.s. pr. cry out.
gruc(c)hen   inf. complain.

halewe   inf. keep holy.
hestes   n. commands.
hoten   pp. be called.
houres   n. observances, canonical hours.

iaapen   3.pl. pr. jest.
ianglen   3.pl. pr. chatter.
iwis(se), ywis, ywysse   adv. certainly.

kepte   3.s. pt. cared.
kynde   n. nature.
kyndely   adv. naturally.

launde   n. clearing.
lay   n. grassland, lawn.
leeche   n. physician.

lesing, leesynges   n. falsehood.
let   n. hindrance.
letten   inf. hinder; letteth, letteþ 3.s. pr.
leue   imp. believe.
leuere   adv. rather.
likerousnesse, lykerousnesse   n. lust.
logge   n. lodging.
lolleris   n. idlers.
loos   n. praise, reputation.
loselis   n. scoundrels.
lother   comp. adj. more reluctant.
lovelyhed   n. humility.
lyflode   n. livlihood.
lyssen   inf. relieve.
lyther   adj. vicious.

maistrie   n. force.
make   n. consort, mate.
maugree   prep. in spite of.
medled   pp. mingled.
meenes   n. intermediaries, agents.
mekil   adj. great.
myscleped   pp. wrongly called.
mysseyn   3.pl. pr. speak badly of.

naturel fool   n. phr. born fool.
not   3.s. pr. does not know.
nyse   adj. foolish.

ocy   imp. kill.

panter   n. fowler's net.
papyngay   n. parrot.
perys   n. equals, nobles.
plesaunce   n. joy.
poudred   pp. flecked, dotted.
pruned   3.pl. pt. preened.

queynte   adj. elaborate, strange.

rage   n. folly, madness.
rather   comp. adj. earlier; raþest sup. adj. soonest.

94

recorde   n. reputation.
rede   inf. advise; rede 1. s. pr.
reeche   imp. care, heed.

sauour   n. pleasure, delight.
sauoure   inf. take pleasure in.
sauoury   adj. delightful.
semelyhed   n. seemliness.
shoopen   3.pl. pr. prepare; shapen pp. destined.
shrewe   1.s. pr. curse.
siker(e), syker   adj. certain.
sikerly, sykerly   adv. certainly, truly.
sithe(n), siþþe(n)   adv. since.
sithe   n. occasions.
skil(l)e(s)   n. reason.
skilfulliche   adv. reasonably.
soth(e)   n. truth.
spille   inf. die.
steigh   3.s. pt. ascended.
sterve   inf. die.
steryng   n. prompting.
stounde   n. moment.
styes   n. steps, paths
swowe   n. swoon.

tacches   n. blemishes.
tene   n. grief, annoyance.
terme   n. duration.
tho   adv. then.
to breke   inf. break in two.
to drowen   3.pl. pt. stretched out.
tokenyng   n. sign, saying.
traaces   n. paths, courses.
trauail(l)(es)   n. hardship.
trauaille   inf. labour; trauaillen 3.pl. pr.

veery   adj. weary.
vneesie   adj. uncomfortable.
vnkynde   adj. unnatural.
vnkyndly   adv. unnaturally.

vnlusty   adj. feeble.
vnlyke   adj. improbable.
vnsauoury   adj. unpleasant.
vnsikere   adj. uncertain.
vnskilful   adj. unreasonable.
vnthrive   3.pl. pr. fail to prosper.
vntrust   n. distrust.
vnworsshipe   n. disgrace.
vsen   3.pl. pr. use, keep as a custom.

wa(c)h(es)   n. lookout.
wacchebrid   n. decoy.
wale   n. valley.
wanhope   n. despair.
weele   n. prosperity.
wem   n. defilement, blemish.
wende   imp. go away.
wight   n. creature.
wo(o)de   adj. mad.
wo(o)d(e)nesse   n. madness.
wonede   3.s. pt. lived.
woot   3.s. pr. knows; wyten 1.pl. pr.
woys   n. voice.

yfeyned   pp. imitated.
ymedled   pp. mingled.
ythe   inf. prosper.